TRIU

OVER

TERROR

Ground Zero Chaplain Bob Ossler
with Janice Hall Heck

BLACKSIDE PUBLISHING

COLORADO SPRINGS, CO

Publisher's Note: This memoir is a work of creative nonfiction. The events are portrayed to the best of Bob Ossler's memory. While all the stories in this book are true, the author tried to recreate events, locales, and conversations from his recollections, though they are not written to represent word-for-word transcripts. Rather, the author retells them in a way to evoke the feeling and meaning of what was said, and in all instances, the essence of the dialogue is accurate. Some names and identifying details were changed to protect the privacy of individuals.

For permission requests, email the publisher at blacksidepublishing@gmail.com: "Attention: Permissions Coordinator."

URL: www.blacksidepublishing.com

Ordering Information: Quantity sales. Special discounts are available on quantity purchases by corporations, associations, and others. For details, email blacksidepublishing@gmail.com

Cover and book design by: Scoti Domeij
Editing by: Katie Allen, Scoti Domeij, Janice Hall Heck
Photos by: Mary Gepana Eble, Scoti Domeij, Dan Pennino, Dan Schafer

Unless otherwise noted, Scripture is taken from the New American Standard Bible ®. Copyright © 1960, 1962, 1963, 1968, 1971, 1972, 1973, 1975, 1977, 1995 by the Lockman Foundation. Used by permission.

Scripture quotations are taken from the Holy Bible, New Living Translation, copyright ©1996, 2004, 2007, 2013, 2015 by Tyndale House Foundation. Used by permission of Tyndale House Publishers, Inc., Carol Stream, Illinois 60188. All rights reserved.

Scripture quotations marked KJV are from the Holy Bible, King James Version (Authorized Version). First published in 1611. Quoted from the KJV Classic Reference Bible, Copyright © 1983 by The Zondervan Corporation.

Printed in the United States of America
Triumph Over Terror/Bob Ossler with Janice Hall Heck
ISBN 13: 978-1-68355-004-4 ISBN 11: 1-68355-004-8
First Edition

Contents

On the 15th anniversary of September 11, 2001,
we remember, honor, and dedicate this book to

... those first responders from the New York Fire Department, the New York Police Department, the New York-New Jersey Port Authority, and the many civilians who lost their lives on September 11, 2001 in New York City, Washington, D.C., and Shanksville, Pennsylvania.

... those first responders, emergency workers, and volunteers, a.k.a. our Ground Zero Heroes, who worked in chaotic, unhealthy, and unsafe conditions immediately after the terrorist attacks to search for survivors, and later, to recover remains of those who lost their lives. Many of these searchers have since passed away due to 9/11-related health issues or now suffer with long-term, life-threatening illnesses.

... the families, friends, and associates of spouses, mothers, fathers, sons, daughters, relatives, friends, and associates who live with wounded hearts and fractured spirits because of their tragic losses of September 11, 2001.

... the citizens of our free country who look forward with hope to lives free from terror.

Together, with God's help, we will triumph over terror.

"Yet those who wait for the LORD
Will gain new strength;
They will mount up with wings like eagles,
They will run and not get tired,
They will walk and not become weary."

—Isaiah 40:31

The Road

While travelling along
it's never too late
Take the road that leads
to Love.
Not the one to hate

Hate is what knocked these
buildings down
With love, we'll remember
those, no longer around
Take the right road
and you will see
how much sweeter
Life will be
The road may be uphill
and strewn with stones
So get rid of the weight
and lighten the load.
AT the summit there
is a beautiful view,

all of God's peace
open to you.

God bless N.Y.C.
+
America
Surviving Police Officer
N.Y.P.P.

Advance Praise for *Triumph Over Terror*

"Triumph Over Terror by Bob Ossler can be summed up in one word: Powerful. We've all seen the images of 9/11. Even though they were hard to look at, we could not turn our eyes away. So I braced myself to read Bob's book, not wanting to remember those images and experience the pain of 9/11 all over again. I intended to take just a minute to see how Bob began his book but got hooked on the first page and just kept reading. *Triumph Over Terror* isn't just a history lesson. It's a book full of life lessons."

—Tim Shoemaker, author of
Super Husband, Super Dad and *The Code of Silence Series*

"I heard Chaplain Bob Ossler speak at Ground Zero at mini-memorial services for those who died on 9-11. I watched him in the aftermath of the loss of the Granite Mountain Hotshots (19 firefighters killed at the Yarnell, AZ wildfires in 2013) where he offered comfort to the immediate family members who lost loved ones. I personally leaned heavily on him after the drowning of a 6-year-old boy in a flash flood in 2010 that I refer to as the most difficult call in my 35-year career. In all of these situations, Chaplain Bob opened himself up to help others deal with the

tragedies that surrounded them. Chaplain Bob is a consummate professional who uses his experiences, faith, and compassion to assist others
in their time of need. I am proud to call him my fellow firefighter, my
Chaplain, and my friend."

—Glenn W. Brown, Fire Chief
Mayer, AZ Fire Department

"Knowing Bob and reading these 9/11 stories in *Triumph Over Terror*
made me imagine being right there with him on the Pile. I'm so proud
that he has gotten to this point of healing that he has been able to write
his memories down in such a powerful yet gentle way. I read and wept
through many of them. Prepare to immerse yourself in Bob's words of
human kindness, inspiration, and compassion."

—Tom Ashcraft, Father of a Granite Mountain
Hot Shot Firefighter killed in 2013 Arizona wildfires

"Chaplain Bob Ossler deserves special honors. He's a man who has
poured out his life in service to others, including the men and women
emergency workers helping put America back together in the aftermath
of 9/11 at Ground Zero. Bob has now written *Triumph Over Terror* about
his experiences during those weeks as he ministered to the hurting. But
his book does not glorify his efforts; instead, it focuses on exalting God
through revealing how God was intimately present in every heartbreaking, weary moment. Bob's book answers the question, "Where was God
during one of our nation's most horrific experiences?"

Triumph Over Terror gives us a glimpse into what it was like to work
at Ground Zero and shows where God is during trials and how He
responds."

—Megan Breedlove, author of *Chaotic Joy:
Finding Abundance in the Messiness of Motherhood*

"I had the blessing of getting to know Chaplain Bob Ossler for a short time as he ministered to workers on the Pile and to families of victims at 9/11's Ground Zero. Chaplain Bob, one of the unsung heroes of 9/11, performed more than 300 mini-services for families who lost loved ones in the 7-story pile of agony that resulted from terrorist attacks. *Triumph Over Terror* takes us back and shows the need for a kinder, gentler world."

—Lesley Visser, Football Hall of Fame Sportscaster

"Chaplain Bob Ossler has been in the rescue business for a long time as a firefighter, paramedic, and ordained minister. He is uniquely gifted in ministering to those who are hurting, so everyone expected him to respond to the call for chaplains after the 9/11 tragedy. But even with all his training and experience in crisis situations, the emotional toll on him was great. When you read *Triumph Over Terror*, you will experience 9/11 in a deeply personal way, and you will see inside the heart of a man who deeply cares for others."

—Sal Roggio, Pastor
Cumberland County Community Church
Millville, New Jersey

"Bob simply lets God's Word and God's love accomplish God's work through him. It is hard to imagine someone with a better set of experiences and expertise for the ministry described in this book. Clearly, God prepared a man for ministry in the immediate aftermath of Ground Zero. That man is Bob Ossler, and *Triumph Over Terror* is his story."

—Steve Kemp, Director of Institutional Partnerships, BILD

"People always want Bob to speak about his experiences at Ground Zero, but few know how hard that is on a person's mental health. I now understand [after the deaths of nineteen firefighters in the Granite Mountain wildfires in Arizona in 2013]. Thank you, Bob, for sharing a wonderful testament to God's glory and our Savior's hand. You have been my inspiration to continue to care for our firefighter families, raise money for the families of 9/11, and honor the words spoken by so many others: 'We will never forget; we remember every day.'"

—Tom Haney, President of the United Yavapai
Firefighters IAFF Local 3066
Vice President of the Professional Firefighters of Arizona (PFFA)
Fire Captain/Paramedic Mayer Fire District, Mayer, Arizona

"I've never met anyone quite like Bob. Since childhood, he has heard the beat to his own drum and has been an original thinker, creative in almost everything he has done, and he's done a ton! Life is difficult at times. Bob has shown courage and compassion. I continue to be inspired by him."

—Tony Patricelli, National Sales Manager,
Dynamex

Foreword

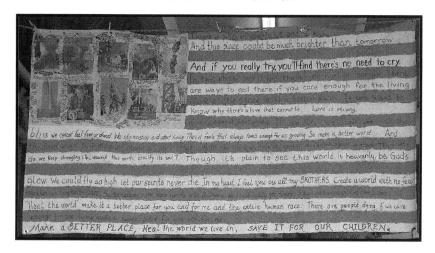

"I don't want to go there."

We've all said those exact words. A painful memory we don't want to dredge up. A journey we're dreading. A place or activity that we sense as being dangerous. Or scary. Or just a little bit creepy.

In the case of remembering the events of September 11, 2001 and the days following, many of us simply don't want to go there. We've been there before—and we don't want to go back. The images of the horror, the carnage, the twisted wasteland of Ground Zero remain seared in our memories.

But we need to look at this devastating tragedy again. We need to remember. We need to go back—but not alone. We need to see the aftermath of 9-11 with the help of a trusted guide. And our guide is Chaplain Bob Ossler.

I first met Bob back in the early 70's, so I've known him many years. Of all the people I've met in my life, Bob is not like any other person I know. He's the king of going places and doing things that others dread, fear, or totally avoid. His career history backs that up.

A Chicago paramedic . . . in the darkest, most volatile projects of the inner city, Bob served in areas so dangerous that he often wore a bulletproof vest when going out on rescue calls. More than once he was attacked by drug-crazed people living in the projects.

A Chicago firefighter . . . rushing into buildings as others ran out.

A rescue diver . . . searching for victims in the ice cold, black waters of Lake Michigan while others stood on shore shivering.

A chaplain and pastor . . . helping people wrestle free from the forces of darkness.

I could go on and talk of other things Bob has done to help others, and tell you stories that would haunt you. He is one of the few men that I would trust with my life. If I were going into a scary or dangerous situation, I'd feel a whole lot better with Bob leading the way.

Which is why Bob is going to lead you safely back to the days immediately following 9-11. While so many of us watched the events in absolute shock and horror and fear, Bob raced to New York City to help. To do what he could do. And he didn't just stay a day or two or three. Bob volunteered for five tours totaling forty-five days in that aftermath.

In *Triumph Over Terror* you'll read stories of daily events, people Bob met, and ultimately life lessons learned in those dark days following 9-11. But more than that, you'll find hope. Healing. Perspective. Renewed strength and courage. And you'll come away with critical life lessons to use as you show compassion and caring to those who suffer.

"I don't want to go there." I know. Nobody does. But you won't go alone. Bob will walk you through the wasteland and bring you out on the other side. That's the kind of thing Bob does. Sometimes it takes someone who's been through the smoke and rubble to help us see our life problems—and solutions—more clearly. I think you'll be glad you took the journey.

You ready? Okay, turn the page.

—Tim Shoemaker, author of eleven books,
including *Super Husband, Super Dad*,
Tim is a speaker at church and writing conferences.

Preface

Writing this book was the hardest work I have ever done. I'm a talker, not a writer. I'm an ordained chaplain, not a psychologist. I love people and want to encourage and support them in times of crisis and need, whenever and wherever the opportunity arises, whatever the mode of communication. And I want to share God's love and comfort with everyone.

I worked at Ground Zero for five tours of duty in the fall of 2001. My first attempts, years ago, to write about September 11, 2001 and its aftermath ended in torrents of tears, frustration, and failure as recalled events tore open unhealed heart wounds. Now, fifteen years later, encouraging writer friends pushed me, yes, even lovingly commanded me to write through the pain, not only to bring closure for myself, but to bring God's message of comfort to others suffering through crises. My friends assured me that my words would encourage others to stand firm in their faith despite heartache and suffering.

"Through sharing our pain," they said, "we touch the hearts of others. So, write out your memories, and let God use them for His purposes."

"But I'm not a writer."

Janice Heck challenged me. "Can you write emails?"

"Yes."

"Then write emails," she suggested.

And so, I began to write again. On this latest attempt, I cried as I wrote out streams of emails, hundreds of them, about random and out-of-order Ground Zero happenings, about memories long buried. These missives soon fell into clusters, then into chapters, then into this book. Incident after incident from Ground Zero flowed back through my mind in startling detail, releasing long pent-up emotions.

But this book is not a retelling of the sequence of happenings on 9/11. *Triumph Over Terror* is my reflection on the tragic assault on New York City and our country and how the hearts and minds of those affected by the events suffered, physically, emotionally, and spiritually. Over time, God helped me and others triumph over this terror to find peace and renewed faith despite the graphic images scrolling through our minds at random times.

Why write another book on 9/11 when so many excellent narratives and documentaries fill bookstore and library shelves? I prayed for emotional closure from long-held distressing memories. But the pain and suffering stirred up by painful flashbacks of traumatic incidents can be redeemed for good. They serve as lessons for others going through heartbreaking, life-altering circumstances.

All of us become counselors at one point or another in our lives. We react to the sorrow of family members, friends, and acquaintances who grieve: a mother loses a child, a spouse loses a partner, a child or adult loses a parent, someone gets badly hurt in an accident, another suffers from addiction, and so on. We acknowledge this hard fact: in this life we will have trouble. We can't escape problems and heartbreak, but with God's help, we can learn resilience. We can triumph over pain and terror, we can recognize the greatness of God, and we can grow in our faith.

Someone greater than us knows the agonies we suffer: Our Heavenly Father watched His only Son die in the most cruelly imaginable way: hanging nailed to a cross in Jerusalem's midday heat. Our Father knows our pain; He experienced it Himself. And Jesus suffered, too. He agonizes with us and offers comfort to us. We, in turn, acknowledge our pain, accept the comfort, then turn and offer this same solace to those around us.

What will readers do with this book? I hope you will read it. Ponder it. Take it to heart. Pass it on to others.

God and Scripture are focal points behind every page. Regardless of the situation, use the many examples, suggestions, and resources as a practical pastoral manual or handy reference to care for others who suffer. People go through difficult times in their lives. They cry and see no solution to life's trials and tribulations. We all face trials, but we can turn to God for comfort. He hears our cries and fulfills the biblical promise: *"When the righteous triumph, there is great glory."* (Proverbs 28:12)

God bless you. Amen.

Bob Ossler

Ground Zero Chaplain

September 11, 2016

Acknowledgements

September 11, 2016

So many people deserve thanks for helping me write this book. First, I thank God. I wasn't sure if I could push through such a difficult emotional task and write these words. I prayed many days and nights as I wrote the stories. I wept as memories haunted me. I remembered the reasons I was afraid to write this book: the panic attacks, the anxiety, the nightmares, the flashbacks, the self-doubt. But God gave me the strength and a refreshed feeling through sharing my words with others and kept me writing.

I thank my wonderful wife, Sue, my very best friend and confidant. She cared for our three daughters, Noelle, Michelle, and Heather while I ministered at Ground Zero. She comforted and encouraged me with her tenderness, her gentle voice, and her loving hugs when she welcomed me home.

My children, Noelle, Michelle, and Heather, were young and didn't understand the situation in New York City, but were overjoyed to see me each time I returned home. Their love was and is strong. What a great feeling.

My mother, Josephine Ossler, who still drives and works in a senior center in Chicago, always said, "Please be careful. I love you." She is a special lady. My sisters, Anne Marie and Linda, and my late brother, Steve, kept a friendly sibling rivalry going with me throughout our growing years, but we encouraged each other to do our best at everything we attempted. My family understood the critical nature of the Ground Zero work and this book-writing venture and encouraged me throughout their duration and after. Families are the best.

My Pastor, Sal Roggio, at Cumberland County Community Church (CCCC) in Millville, New Jersey, where I serve as Pastor of Visitation and Evangelism, urged me to join the writer's group held in the church and pushed me to move forward on this writing project. Thanks to Kathryn Ross, Bruce E. Puckett, Ron Newman, Stacy Morrow Zeiger, Janice Heck, and Sal Roggio, members of the group who heard my stories. They demanded that I write them out, encouraged me when I faltered, and urged me to write through the painful memories.

Thanks to my editor/writer/friend Janice Heck. This fine woman took my stories from hundreds of my emails, organized and polished them, and made them worthy of being on the pages of this book. She took my jumbled cacophony of words and made them sing. We spent hours and hours together reviewing the email blasts as she insisted on more details, then consoled me when those details poured salt in my open wounds.

My CCCC writers group challenged me to attend the 2015 Greater Philadelphia Christian Writers Conference organized by Marlene Bagnull where editors, publishers, and other writers read drafts of this manuscript and encouraged me to keep writing. I was overwhelmed and humbled by the enthusiastic response I received from professionals and conference attendees alike.

Our editor/publisher, Scoti Springfield Domeij from Blackside Publishing, grasped the intent and focus as well as the heart and soul of the book on reading the first proposal. She urged me to write more and to submit a manuscript for review. Her enthusiasm pushed us to complete the project, and her editorial assistance has been superb. Surely God planned for us to meet. I also want to thank Scoti for writing *Where Was God in the Wreckage?* Katie Allen added her editorial expertise and helped us tighten the narrative.

Photographers also contributed their talents to this book: Chaplain Dan Schafer shared photos from his private collection taken at Ground Zero. He is a renowned chaplain trainer and works extensively all over the USA. Dan Pennino, friend and CCCC member, provided still shots of my 9/11 artifacts. Mary Gepana Eble and Chaplain Dan Schafer provided photos they shot at Ground Zero and on the streets around Ground Zero in the days immediately after September 11, 2001.

Finally, thanks to the readers who gave feedback and encouraged me to continue writing: Tom Ashcraft, Megan Breedlove, Glenn W. Brown, Tom Haney, Janean Haney, Steve Kemp, Tony Patricelli, Tim Shoemaker, Lesley Visser, Joe Orazi, and Connie Swanson. You are all special friends. Your encouragement touched my heart.

As I worked at Ground Zero through five tours of duty, I saw the good, the bad, and the ugly, but I gained new respect and love for people and life. Through that miserable, heart-breaking, and devastating experience, I learned to appreciate people more, to hold my family closer, and to keep in touch with friends old and new.

Terrorism tried to destroy our lives, but we triumphed over terror, just as Romans 8:37-39 promised: *"But in all these things we overwhelmingly conquer through Him who loved us. For I am convinced that neither death, nor life, nor angels, nor principalities, nor things present, nor things to come, nor powers, nor height, nor depth, nor any other created thing, will be able to separate us from the love of God, which is in Christ Jesus our Lord."*

God blessed me through the writing of this book. The terrorists didn't win. I have conquered my nightmarish 9/11 memories through Him who loves me, and I've grown stronger in my faith. Terror no longer has me in its grips. You, too, can find that peace in our Lord.

Give someone a hug today and be blessed. Amen.

Chaplain Bob Ossler

Prologue

"Today, our fellow citizens, our way of life, our very freedom came under attack in a series of deliberate and deadly terrorist acts. The victims were in airplanes or in their offices: secretaries, businessmen and women, military and federal workers, moms and dads, friends and neighbors. Thousands of lives suddenly ended by evil, despicable acts of terror. The pictures of airplanes flying into buildings, fires burning, and huge—huge structures collapsing have filled us with disbelief, terrible sadness, and a quiet, unyielding anger. These acts of mass murder were intended to frighten our nation into chaos and retreat. But they have failed. Our country is strong."

—President George W. Bush, September 11, 2001

On September 11, 2001, an estimated 10,000 to 14,000 people arrived at the World Trade Center (WTC) in New York City before 8:45 a.m. to start their workday. At 8:46 a.m., their day ended in chaos. With a force equal to 480,000 pounds of TNT, terrorists slammed a fully fueled Boeing 767, traveling at 494 mph, into the 93rd through 99th floors on the north side of 1 World Trade Center trapping everyone above the 92nd floor. Burning jet fuel flowed down elevator shafts. When elevator doors opened at the 78th floor and ground floor lobbies, fireballs blasted into crowds of people waiting to escape.

At 9:03 a.m., a second commercial airliner, flying at 586 mph slammed into 2 World Trade Center, the South Tower, striking on an angle between the 77th and 85th floors.

These once majestic 110-story skyscrapers, now flaming and smoldering, remained standing, but not for long. The intense heat of the jet-fueled fires weakened the steel support trusses in both buildings. At 9:50 a.m., forty-seven minutes after impact, amid thunderous noise and in a hellish storm of steel beams, pulverized cement, and shattered glass, 2 World Trade Center, the South Tower, pancaked, layer by layer, crushing everything and everyone remaining in the building: hundreds of moms, dads, sisters and brothers, relatives, friends, and associates.

At 10:29 a.m., 1 World Trade Center, the North Tower plummeted down into a 70-foot high pile of rubble. Enormous pieces of the building façade projected upward from the debris, and silhouetted haphazardly tilted against the sky.

Inside the smoking avalanche of steel and concrete, a small section of stairwell A remained intact. A small group of firefighters and three civilians huddled there, trapped but alive.

In one hundred and two minutes, less than two hours after the initial attack, the terrorist *fait accompli* destroyed the twin towers and seriously damaged the World Trade Center 16-acre complex.

According to the 9/11 Memorial Museum FAQ, on September 11, 2001 nearly 3000 people from 93 nations were killed: 2,753 in New York City, 184 at the Pentagon and 40 people near Shanksville, PA.

Located on 16 acres of prime land in the Financial District of Lower Manhattan in New York City, seven buildings composed the World Trade Center complex (WTC). Church Street, Vesey Street, West Street, and Liberty Street formed the boundaries of the WTC buildings. The twin Towers, 1 WTC and 2 WTC, rising 1,368 feet into the sky overshadowed other low-rise buildings, WTC buildings 3, 4, 5, 6, and 7.

The 9/11 Memorial Museum historical exhibition states the WTC ruins towered 70 feet high, not including the stories-tall façade impaled in the wreckage. Destruction and debris extended out to Broadway, Chambers Street, the Hudson River, and Rector Street. The debris mound called "The Pile" included: twisted steel beams, shattered glass, giant chunks of broken concrete, pulverized sheetrock, bent rebar, miles of twisted cable and wire, and smashed office furniture and equipment.

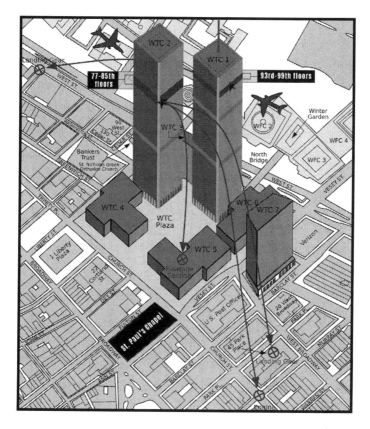

Defined by barricades and chain link fences, the perimeter bordering the debris field ensured the security of workers and visitors to the area. At multiple stations along the perimeter, National Guard personnel checked credentials of workers entering the Pile. Search and rescue workers initially scoured the highly unsafe, unstable, super-heated, still smoking trash Pile for survivors, but found only a few. When all hope for survivors diminished, search and recovery teams looked for human remains to be identified through DNA and returned to families for proper burial.

Within days of the 9/11 terrorist attacks, a call to action was issued for chaplains to come to New York City to help the first responders and families of those who lost loved ones cope with traumatic experiences associated with the tragedy. This is where my story begins.

September 11, 2001

7:50 a.m.: American Airlines, AA#11, departs Boston's Logan International Airport (BOS) for Los Angeles International Airport (LAX). On board: 81 passengers and 11 crew members.

8:14 a.m.: United Airlines UAL#175 departs BOS headed to LAX with 56 passengers and 9 crew members.

8:20 a.m.: AA #77 departs Washington, D.C. for LAX with 58 passengers and 6 crew members.

8:42 a.m.: UAL #93 departs Newark Liberty International Airport (EWR) for San Francisco, CA (SFO) with 37 passengers and 7 crew members.

8:46 a.m.: Terrorists plow hijacked AA#11 into the north side of 1 WTC.

9:02 a.m.: South Tower occupants told to evacuate, but many had already evacuated. Evacuation order issued, but not everyone heard it.

9:03 a.m.: UAL #175 slams airplane into south side of 2 WTC.

9:15 a.m.: Officials begin closing New York City bridges and tunnels to all but emergency vehicles and pedestrians.

9:25 a.m.: The Federal Aviation Administration (FAA) orders first-ever nationwide ground-stop, prohibiting flight departures from U.S. airports.

9:37 a.m.: Hijackers crash AA#77 into Pentagon.

9:40 a.m.: FAA orders 4546 airplanes in the North American airspace to land at the nearest airport.

By 9:45 a.m.: Evacuations ordered at White House and Capitol in Washington, D.C., and major sites around the country, including the United Nations, Disney World, and Kennedy Space Center.

9:59 a.m.: 2 WTC, the South Tower, 110 floors collapse in 9 seconds. Building debris falls on Marriott Hotel causing severe damage.

10:03 a.m.: Hijackers crash UAL#93 in a field in Shanksville, Pennsylvania, after passengers try to seize control of the aircraft.

10:28 a.m.: 1 WTC, North Tower, 110 floors collapse in 11 seconds damaging surrounding WTC buildings. All 16 acres of the World Trade Center site in ruins.

10:30 a.m.: New York Governor George E. Pataki declares a state of emergency in New York state.

10:50 a.m.: One five-story high section of the Pentagon collapses in Washington, D.C.

11:02 a.m.: In New York City Mayor Rudolph Giuliani orders evacuation of Lower Manhattan below Canal Street, including workers, residents, tourists, and schoolchildren.

1:27 a.m.: State of Emergency declared in Washington, D.C.

8:30 p.m.: President Bush addresses the nation.

SECTION 1

The Gates of Hell

"Lord, take me where You want me to go; let me meet who You want me to meet; tell me what You want me to say; and keep me out of Your way."

—Father Mychal Judge
Holy Name Province
Order of Friars Minor
Franciscan Friars, New York

1

Compelled to Help in Any Way I Can

"The place God calls you to is the place where your deep gladness and the world's deep hunger meet."

—Parker Palmer

September 12, 2001

"Hey Bob, did you hear the news?"

Max, my six-foot-tall Chicago Fire Department Air Sea Rescue diving partner, threw his sopping sponge at me as we finished washing down our helicopter at Meigs Field, Chicago's beautiful landmark, lakefront airport. "New York City authorities put out a call for chaplains at Ground Zero. You gonna go?"

I set down my drying chamois and leaned against the now gleaming chopper. The day before, I watched with the rest of the country as the World Trade Center towers fell. I looked at Max and said, "I'm going."

My varied training and work experience prepared me for disaster relief. With experience as a firefighter, paramedic, and ordained chaplain, I often faced severely traumatized people in the worst moments of their lives. My fire fighting and paramedic training prepared me for the physical side of critical incidents and disaster relief, but my chaplaincy training emphasized the interpersonal nature of working with emotionally and spiritually wounded people. My Christian faith prompted me to reach out to offer comfort and a glimmer of hope to those suffering in this tragedy.

First, though, I needed to talk to Sue, my dear wife. But even before I broached the topic of heading to New York City to help in the aftermath of the terrorist attacks, she sensed I wanted to go. She held her concerns for my health and safety to herself and agreed I should respond to the call.

"God prepared you for this crisis," Sue said. "You need to go. The girls and I will be fine. Just be careful."

I'd only be away for a week or two at a time. Nearby family members promised to pitch in to help with my three daughters Noelle, Michelle, and Heather when needed. Confident my wife would cover me in prayer throughout my time away, I began my preparations.

Volunteers at critical incidents often use personal accumulated vacation time at their regular jobs and rotate in and out of on-site service based on breaks in their primary work schedules. I scrambled to trade my scheduled shifts at the Chicago Fire Department, and I patched together enough leave time to cover two weeks away.

I packed my black rolling carry-on suitcase and donned my thirty pounds of turnout gear: a heavy black waterproof firefighter's coat with Melrose Park Fire Department and CHAPLAIN OSSLER emblazoned across the back, heavy work boots, and my white chaplain's hard hat.

Wearing my clerical collar, I headed to Chicago O'Hare International Airport. On September 11 at 9:25 a.m. (EDT) twenty-two minutes after the second plane hit the World Trade Center, the Department of Transportation shut down the airspace across the United States and reopened the airspace on 11 a.m. on September 13. By the time I was in transit to the airport, some commercial flights were taking off again. I purchased a ticket to New York City.

Other travelers recognized my outfit and guessed my destination. Complete strangers approached me, tears in their eyes, wanting to shake my hand and to express their sorrow about the loss of so many lives in the devastation at the World Trade Center. They asked me to carry their prayers for comfort to New Yorkers.

Some headed to New York City themselves to check on family, friends, or work associates they hadn't heard from since 9/11. *Where were they? Had they been in those towers when they collapsed? Were they alive or dead?* These frightened travelers didn't know what to expect.

Many asked me to pray for them and with them: "Father God, thank You for being our awesome God. Please protect these folks as they fly to New York City to find their missing friends. Help them be strong in their emotions and tender spirited around those who hurt. Surround their hearts and minds with an angelic hedge to protect them from the overwhelming trauma and suffering we'll all see in New York City. In Your name, Jesus Christ, we pray. Amen."

One man responded to my prayer. "Chaplain, can we pray for you?"

"Yes, of course."

"Dear Father, protect Chaplain Bob's family when he is far from home. Keep him in good health and sound mind as he works in this dangerous situation. Help him be Your faithful servant as he touches their lives with Your bountiful love. Guide him safely home again when his work ends. Amen."

This man's prayer touched my apprehensive heart, giving me courage to continue on this risky venture.

After disembarking the plane at Newark Liberty International Airport, I exited the airport and approached a police officer directing traffic. "Officer, can you point me to a bus that will take me to Ground Zero?"

The officer looked sideways at me. "Why are you headed to the towers?"

I set down my carry-on suitcase on the sidewalk and turned so he could read the lettering on the back of my firefighter's jacket. "I'm a Chicago fire department firefighter and a chaplain in Melrose, Illinois. I'm trying to get to Ground Zero to see if I can help."

His expression shifted. He looked over my hefty turnout gear, and said, "Follow me." I trailed close behind as he led me to the closest waiting bus—already stuffed with passengers. The officer leaned in to speak to the driver. "Take this chaplain down to Ground Zero."

The driver stared at the officer. "You serious? I got fourteen miles to cover. See this?" He gestured to the packed bus. "All of these folks are headed to different places. Manhattan is way out of my way and theirs too. It's gridlock in Manhattan at this time of day, and it gets worse the closer you get to Ground Zero." The driver shrugged.

I glanced at the passengers. "Can you get me relatively near the area? I'll walk the rest of the way."

One man sitting near the front of the bus leaned forward and motioned for me to board the bus. "Come on, Chaplain. We'll take you."

The passengers murmured. Several more yelled agreement from the back of the bus.

"So it takes a little longer," the first man added. "So what?"

The driver nodded his head. "Okay, let's get going."

I pulled my wallet out of my pocket, and he waved it away, red-faced. "No charge, Chaplain."

The riders welcomed me on the bus and found me a seat. They didn't mind that they'd arrive at their journeys' ends much later than expected. They wanted to do their part to help out at Ground Zero.

As the bus pulled out of the airport, they barraged me with the same questions swirling in my mind since I'd decided to come on this venture:

"What will you do here?" "Where will you stay?" "How long will you be here?"

"Well," I said. "I don't have answers to all your questions, but I trust that God will provide for my needs. I'm here to do whatever needs to be done, and I want to spread hope wherever I can by sharing God's love and grace." I asked, "Can I pray with all of you."

The passengers accepted, and even offered prayers of their own. As we spoke in turns, our eyes filled with tears. We praised God for all the help arriving in this traumatized city. The openness of all those strangers—and their willingness to pray aloud—amazed me. Praying in public, I soon learned, was the new norm in New York City.

People asked for prayer. People offered prayer. *Everywhere.*

At first, the bus driver feared driving too close to Ground Zero and tried to drop me off miles away. His passengers persuaded him to move closer. At one point, the bumper-to-bumper traffic ground to a complete stop.

Concrete barriers blocked streets and police officers waved vehicles away from Ground Zero. Pedestrians jammed the sidewalks, trying to maneuver around barriers to a thousand destinations. Around us, short-tempered, frazzled drivers pounded on their horns, adding to the ungodly pandemonium. Smog hung in the air above the city.

About a half-mile before the blockaded perimeter of Ground Zero, I told the bus driver to stop. "I can hop off here and walk the rest of the way."

I exchanged heartfelt goodbyes with my new friends and hopped off the bus. Even though heavy ash permeated the air and left a strange taste in my mouth, I breathed without difficulty and set off dragging my wheeled suitcase behind me.

Navigating to Ground Zero required great effort. Whole streets, blocked off to vehicles and

pedestrians alike, created an enormous maze. The acrid smoky smell of carnage filled the air. Layers of ash, inches thick, coated everything in sight: trash cans, mangled cars with windshields blown out and paint blasted off, topless thin trees poking out of the sidewalk. As I moved closer to the site, the chaos and noise of Manhattan died into near-reverential quiet. Only the occasional wail of a siren interrupted my odyssey of mercy. I zigzagged through this giant morass in full firefighting gear, worried that those in charge might not even let me help.

Scrambled thoughts flooded my mind. *What am I doing here in this madness? How will I find food and water? Where can I plug in my cell phone so I can call my wife?*

Still daylight, I found all kinds of volunteers standing in a line stretching for blocks. *Who are these people? Construction workers? Rescue workers? Emergency responders?* Wearing a hodgepodge of partial uniforms and hefting bags of gear, it was hard to tell what each hoped to accomplish. Feeling helpless at the enormity of the situation, we all just wanted to stand in line and be assigned a task to help in some way.

I joined the line and waited for about an hour with no movement at all. Then one police officer noticed my clerical collar and called to me. "Hey buddy. The clergy line is over here." He motioned me to a separate, shorter line.

At the head of this new line, three officials in dusty uniforms sat at a table interviewing each person checking in. Minutes later, I reached the head of the line, and they peppered me with questions: "Do you have a photo ID and credentials?" They verified my identification. "What is your purpose for coming to Ground Zero?"

"I'm here to help in any way I can and to offer comfort to families and friends of loved ones who were killed in this tragedy."

Satisfied with my answers, one of the officials cautioned, "We have a few guidelines for chaplains. Follow them, and you will be welcome here. If not, you'll be asked to leave. No proselytizing. You are here to offer comfort and not to convert. Respect people's privacy. Offer to talk to people, but if they refuse your invitation, leave them alone. Don't preach at them. When people ask, be ready to offer prayer and answer their questions."

I agreed to their conditions. That's the way I worked anyway. As I walked to join some chaplains already cleared by the authorities, I prayed: *"Thank You, Lord, for getting me here safely and helping me connect with other chaplains here in New York City. Watch over Sue and my girls while I'm away. Now, Lord, can You help me find a place to stay? Thank You in advance for Your answer, Lord."*

Within minutes, a young, dark-haired woman dressed in faded jeans, a plaid shirt, and boots approached our small group of chaplains.

"Welcome to New York City, chaplains. And thank you for offering to help us here. I'm a rabbinical student," she said. "I'm taking time off from my studies to volunteer with the rescue and relief efforts. I'll take you to St. Paul's Chapel where we'll give you food and shelter while you minister at Ground Zero."

As we walked to our temporary living quarters, the woman talked over her shoulder, "St. Paul's Chapel has changed its regular ministry and turned the church into a respite center for workers and volunteers. It will stay open as long as it's needed for the 9/11 cleanup." She stopped and looked at us again. "We're happy to have all of you here. Now prepare yourselves for the worst things you've ever seen or will ever see again. Use your faith to keep you whole. God bless you for coming to assist us in coping with this American tragedy. You bring hope to our crushed hearts and our broken city."

Again I silently prayed. *Thank You, Lord. You're an awesome God. Thank You for answering my prayers so quickly for food and a place to stay. Now embrace us in Your loving arms and keep us safe from harm as we minister to those in physical, emotional, and spiritual need. Help me to reflect Your love in this dreadful time and place.*

2

Missing Persons:
Have You Seen Me?

"...New torments and new tormented souls I see around me wherever I move, and howsoever I turn, and wherever I gaze."

— Dante Alighieri, *Inferno. Canto VI*

Walking the short distance to St. Paul's Chapel, we encountered the somber evidence of the huge number of people who died in the World Trade Center. Frantic, grief-stricken loved ones in confusion and disbelief plastered photos and flyers for missing persons everywhere around the perimeter of Ground Zero and Lower Manhattan: fluttering posters covered buildings, lampposts, fences, pillars, and windows; signs hung on chain link fences, even blocking existing ads on kiosks and subway walls. Inside St. Paul's Chapel, more pictures hung on the walls, columns, and stairwell and balcony railings.

All sizes, colors, and shapes of signs. Hand-written and computer-printed. Hand-drawn and crayon-colored pictures by children. Photo collages of missing persons. Pictures of firefighters and police officers in uniform. Multi-generation family pictures. Photos of men and women, young and old. Thousands of pictures. All loved ones missing in this vast destruction.

Endless names flashed through my mind as we passed the posters—David, Christopher, Cal, John, Marilyn, Christina, Dennis, Jose, Kevin,

Manuel, Mary Lou, Andre, Leah, Demetrius, Anthony, Sean, Carlos, Matt, Darelia, Terence, Carol, Ramon—on and on, down the rows and rows and columns of pictures and posters papering the buildings along the streets. These makeshift missing person reports tore at my heart and tears flooded my eyes.

Missing: Last Seen at the World Trade Center on September 11.

Have you seen my Daddy? A photo of child and father in a park.

Have you seen my son? He worked on the 94th floor of Tower 1. Call me.

Here's a picture of my sister, and I'm proud to show her to the world.

A picture of a man and his small son. *My dad is missing, and we want him back.*

Removed from me in body, but never far from my heart. A wedding photo.

We miss you!

Sun . . . wind . . . overnight dampness . . . curled the edges of weather-faded pictures and flyers. Rain-streaked inks trailed muddy tears down the printed faces. Garish images created by the physical changes added to the sadness of the scene.

One picture showed a smiling family man with his children; another, a lovely young woman who looked full of life and happiness. I imagined these missing people with their families on happy occasions—birthdays, anniversaries, graduations, holidays—or just alive and well in  their everyday activities. This sobering walk by the photos offered time to reflect and honor each person lost.

Photos of women my wife's age caught my attention. *What if Sue had worked in one those towers?* I'd plaster thousands of pictures of her on every street lamp, fence post, and building wall in town, hoping against hope to find her alive. I took a moment to thank God for her constant love and presence in my life and for her safety at home.

Suffering acute pain not knowing if their missing loved ones were alive or dead, family members and friends posted these heartbreaking photos, hoping and praying for miracles. Hundreds of pedestrians walked by these missing person signs, often stopping and paying their respects in silence.

Some prayed.

Many cried.

Others shook their heads in disbelief.

A middle-aged gentleman placed his hand on a photo of a young man in a business suit and tie, bowed his head, and leaned toward the wall. His shoulders heaved with sobs of agony. His son died in one of the WTC collapsed towers.

An elderly woman stood before the pictures, handkerchief in hand covering her mouth, as if to say, "Oh my, how can this even be possible?"

These informal, impromptu displays symbolized the fight for us, as a people, as a nation: a pictorial memorial of those we lost. These *"Have you seen...?"* pictures represented the last hope for the families, delaying the unthinkable—their loved ones—killed in the Twin Towers.

During my tours at Ground Zero, I stopped often at these paper memorials and prayed for the families of the missing persons. I asked God to give them peace, for resilience to go on without their loved ones, and for others to support them in their loss.

In times of tragedy and deep mourning, all chaplains or encouragers can offer is their presence, a listening ear, and prayer. Just as God draws near to the brokenhearted and the crushed in spirit, I prepared my heart to draw near and listen as they talked about their pain. And when an appropriate moment opened, I offered words of comfort from the Bible as part of my prayer. God cares about our pain and bears our hardship with us, just as the psalmist expressed in Psalm 46:1-2: *"God is our refuge and strength, a very present help in trouble. Therefore we will not fear, though the earth should change and the mountains slip into the heart of the sea . . . "*

3

Sweeper Man's Hopeless Task

"I must lose myself in action, lest I wither in despair."
—Alfred Lord Tennyson

Soon after our introduction to St. Paul's staff, another volunteer offered to take us on an orientation tour of Ground Zero. As I walked with about twenty other chaplains toward the smoky, smoldering, stories-high wreckage of buildings and souls, we passed a fatherly-looking figure pushing a long-handled broom. A dirty sweatshirt barely covered his protruding belly. White chalky ash shrouded his pant legs—the pulverized cement of collapsed buildings intermingled with ashes of cremated bodies. Engulfed in the stench of death, he swept and pushed, swept and pushed at piles of dust-fine ash and dirt, twisted metal and broken glass, chunks of concrete, tangled wires, and papers blown from the demolished towers. Debris stretched as far the eye could see, endless—but still Sweeper Man swept and pushed, swept and pushed.

To restore order to his street, one man faced the greatest physical and emotional challenge of his lifetime. He picked up his broom to do something, *anything,* no matter how small.

Swoosh, swoosh. Swoosh, swoosh—a symbol of hope. He pushed his long-handled broom slowly but steadily, shoving away the rubble and ash of shattered buildings and lives.

As our group of chaplains walked by on Sweeper Man's newly created pathway, he stepped aside. We greeted him, and he nodded.

After we passed him, I looked back. He leaned on his broom, lowered his head, and started to cry. In that overwhelming mess, he looked so forlorn trying to clean his patch of the city he loved. Seeing him weep over his broom broke my heart.

I walked back and embraced him. He grabbed onto me and sobbed on my shoulder. "I'm exhausted from trying to clean up this mess. It's hopeless. Hopeless. Hopeless."

I hugged him harder and complimented him on his nice, clean area, and how much I appreciated the time and effort he invested into clearing the trash and junk away. Before I moved back to the group of chaplains, I offered to share a prayer with him. He accepted, so we prayed together and asked God for strength in these terrible times.

Sweeper Man thanked me for the hug, the prayer, and the encouragement. After I turned to catch up to my group, he went back to work with his broom to make his path wider—sweeping, sweeping.

A tragedy of unspeakable proportions left his little corner of New York City totally trashed, but he persevered at his work.

Steady. Reliable. Crushed in spirit, but buoyed with enough encouragement to begin again, to take one more step, to push the broom one more time, to sweep away at the ruins threatening to bury all hope.

I was glad I'd turned back to acknowledge his pain. After all, that's why I left home and journeyed to New York City: to bring a touch of God's love to the brokenhearted. I remembered something Henri Nouwen wrote in his book, *The Wounded Healer*: "One eye movement or one handshake can replace years of friendship when man is in agony. Love not only lasts forever, it needs only a second to come about." Even though I may never see Sweeper Man again, for one moment in time, our lives connected, and God's love touched us both. I'll never forget him.

Sweeper Man reminded me of an important lesson that day: No matter the job, every single person who works in disaster cleanup is important and needs to be appreciated and recognized for their efforts. When everything appears overwhelming, each individual needs encouragement to keep on doing their job.

4

102 Minutes That
Changed the World

"Through me you go into a city of weeping . . . through me you go amongst the lost people."

—Dante Alighieri, *The Inferno*

Spielberg's outdone himself. Crazy first thought? Yes, but . . . this was real life and real death, not a movie set. Somehow, viewing this 16-acre apocalyptic spectacle as a Hollywood set prevented the harsh reality of this tragedy from overwhelming me.

Jumbled concrete chunks disarranged like the ruins of an ancient civilization; the fog of smoke and ash drifted over the trucks and volunteers; offensive odors assaulted my lungs. . . .

I needed to keep my emotions in check to be effective in my work. And so I kept repeating the words in my mind: *This is just a movie set.*

Our guide turned and looked over the small group of chaplains following his lead. "Welcome to the Gates of Hell."

The gates of what?

That statement jarred me to my inner core, scaring me witless. Our guide's description was definitely not scripturally sound. Hell cannot be portrayed in Hollywood terms or set designs. But as I walked and viewed the destruction and mayhem fueled by ten violent, suicidal Islamic extremist terrorists, I grasped from a feeble human's point of view what hell might look, smell, and even taste like. An overbearing stench—the incense of hell—wafted from the Pile.

We walked onto "The Pile,"—the name rescue workers dubbed the mess at the center of Ground Zero. The top layers quivered beneath our feet. Heavy equipment worked to pull steel girders and beams free from the ruins. A constant reminder of the fragility of the debris stacked haphazardly beneath us, the shaking, rattling movement vibrated like an earthquake deep in the chasms and faults below. We stepped carefully around the crevices and gaping pits lest we lose our balance and plunge into the voids created by the collapsed Twin Towers. I never felt safe on that unstable pile.

How did so much devastation happen in only 102 minutes? Just seven days before, on September 11, 2001 shortly after 9:00 a.m., as first responders ran toward the burning North Tower, many to their deaths, I sauntered through the lobby of a downtown Chicago build-ing on just another nor-mal, uneventful Tuesday. A group of strangely hushed people stood gaping at a TV in the corner.

Wow! Oprah must have an amazing celebrity line-up scheduled for today. I chuckled as I imagined Oprah interviewing a world-famous personal-ity—maybe a glamorous Hollywood star or a crafty politician. Maybe the current hot-shot, weight-loss guru.

The eerie silence of the crowd intrigued me. *What's on TV that's cap-tivating their interest? It can't be Oprah.* I wandered over to check out what mesmerized the onlookers. What I saw on that screen froze my heart. A commercial airplane rammed into and through a skyscraper. Fireballs and dense black smoke broiled from the building. In the background, smoke poured from a second tower.

This was no accident. Two commercial airplanes crashing into the WTC Twin Towers on a bright, clear fall day? No. Not possible. Unthinkable.

As spectators, we stared in helpless astonishment as people engulfed by fire and smoke in New York City lost their lives. The scream of whistling metal slamming into two major landmark buildings meant only one thing: A terror attack in the heart of America.

We stood stock-still as people burned to death or leapt to their deaths to escape stifling smoke and steel-melting heat. We held our breath in silence as we watched video loops recycle unimaginable scenes too horrendous to digest.

Mingled disbelief, shock, and horror overloaded every viewer transfixed by this live-streamed, televised demarcation between lighthearted entertainment and a national living nightmare. Crushing fear gripped our hearts and minds, yet our eyes remained glued to the television.

Our world will never be the same again.

In 102 minutes the terrorist's *fait accompli* destroyed the 16-acre World Trade Center complex.

This is real.

And this is happening right now.

And that's not all. At 9:37 a.m., a third hijacked plane crashed into the five-story Pentagon Building in Washington, D.C. At 10:03 a.m., a fourth plane crashed into a field in Pennsylvania, brought down by courageous American citizens who realized the hijackers planned to attack our nation's key government buildings.

No one ever imagined terrorist attacks of this magnitude in our country. And certainly no one expected a series of well-coordinated attacks by airplanes, now weapons of mass destruction, on core landmarks of our country, the financial center in New York City and our government center in Washington, D.C.

Along with Americans and people around the world, I witnessed the terror attack and resulting aftermath live on TV. We saw the towers buckle and plunge straight down. A billowing shock wave of smoke surged down the streets, chasing terror-stricken, ash-coated people running for their lives.

We heard awful things: hundreds of firefighters killed in the collapse, thousands of WTC workers smashed beyond recognition, desperate humans jumping from the towers. We saw the crush of people in dirty clothing clambering to board ferries and boats descending on The Battery in Lower Manhattan to rescue and move people to safety. We watched the destruction on TV, but still, our minds failed to comprehend the enormity of the devastation.

Arriving onsite at Ground Zero seven days after 9/11 proved to be even more gut-twisting, stomach-churning, and heart-wrenching. The televised images, however wretched, came nowhere near those first-hand smells, tastes, and sensations. Acrid smoke and toxic steam rose from fires raging underground. Putrefying bodies, few intact, remained trapped beneath the rubble. Choking, swirling dust and pulverized concrete mixed with DNA coated our tongues with grit. Hot metal seared through our thick-soled, leather work boots. Everything we touched—debris, trash, and yes, human bones, body parts, and pieces of flesh—fused themselves into memories that refused to leave.

But I was not even a first responder. I was not there in the minutes after the towers crashed to the ground. None of the awfulness I saw on TV compared to the horror those first responders reported. Cameras captured shocking scenes, but panned away to avoid the worst of the sights and sounds. But those first responders saw it all. They bore the brunt of the fear and trauma.

Their stories, vivid in detail, sickened my stomach: men and women plummeting ninety stories to escape the burning jet fuel, heat and choking smoke, disintegrating on impact into flesh and exposed bone as they struck concrete sidewalks or the roof of the adjacent 22-story Marriott Hotel. I prayed for the brave individuals who witnessed the desperate jumpers. *Hold them in Your arms, God, and comfort them. Shield their minds and hearts from the horror they've witnessed.*

First responders, police officers, firefighters, and paramedics, rushed into the scene to save people and to extinguish the fires. But how could firefighters control flames started by nearly 24,000 gallons of jet fuel? How could they fight a conflagration of hellish proportions, eighty-plus stories up in the sky, beyond the reach of the tallest hook-and-ladder fire trucks and the longest fire hoses?

As I stood in horror in front of that TV on 9/11, I thought of those terrorists who didn't value the sacredness of life and counted their success in dead bodies and mass murder. Terrorists, who believed violence to be acceptable to achieve their ends, slaughtered several thousand people from all walks of life. Husbands lost wives; wives lost husbands. Children orphaned. Families destroyed. The financial district shattered. Our country thrown into shock. The hideousness of senseless terrorism surpassed sane human thinking.

This surreal, Spielberg-like scene really *was* a sliver of hell. In the midst of the shock, a whirlwind of questions reverberated through my heart: *Will there be more attacks? How could this happen in our great country?*

In the face of so much tragedy and suffering, many questioned, "Where was God? Why did God let this happen?"

Now as I stared at the piled remains of the WTC towers, I vowed to do my best to bring the love of Jesus here—and that vow, my friends, involved an enormous amount of prayer. Even now, years later, I shudder when I think about the Gates of Hell at Ground Zero.

I prayed for our country and for our future. *God bless America. Lord help us overcome this tragedy. Help us find beauty and truth again and triumph over terror. Thank You, God.*

5

What on Earth Am I
Doing in This Hell?

"There is no center to this day, no middle or end. All its remaining minutes and hours . . . collapsed into that single instant at 8:48 a.m."

—Dennis Smith, *Report from Ground Zero*

As a paramedic and a firefighter, I'd seen gruesome scenes at traffic accidents and burning buildings. Even so, apprehension gripped me as we entered the debris field at Ground Zero. I stopped and prayed for safety and protection, both for my mind and body, for the other volunteers, and for everyone involved in the ominous cleanup work.

At first, what I saw at Ground Zero made no sense at all. Adjacent to the now-former site of the Twin Towers, I saw the 41-story Deutsche Bank, bearing a 20-story gouge where part of 2 WTC, the South Tower, rammed down into it. It appeared as if a humongous creature had clawed out a great chunk of the building. And now, a huge piece of façade from the fallen South Tower dangled precariously from the bottom edge of the gash. Ghostly office furniture, file cabinets, and desks, stood frozen in time in that open-air, cutaway of the damaged building.

Construction workers high up on cranes and cherry-pickers attempted to cut the heavy steel framework of the dangling fragment with blowtorches to prevent it from crashing down on the search and rescue teams below. Deafening industrial sounds filled the air—crashing, banging, hammering, slamming, and beeping of heavy equipment moving in reverse.

Surreal. Destruction everywhere. Five hundred degree toxic smoke and steam rose where the towers once touched to the sky. Heavy machinery dragged and pulled scrap steel beams from the Pile. Semi-sized dump trucks lined up to take endless loads of debris offsite. Once-beautiful, iconic skyscrapers soared high above Manhattan's skyline—now lay in heaping mounds of trash.

Nothing recognizable remained in the towering debris pile: no carpeting, no fixtures, no furniture, no file cabinets, no personal framed photos, nothing . . . except one single intact sign. It read, "You are here."

Fighter jets patrolled the skies overhead. Only days before I'd taken for granted our safety and security as Americans. But this devastating act of terrorism triggered everyone's emotional emergency warning systems, seizing our awareness with the urgency to protect our country. The distinctive whine, whoosh, and roar of their jet engines sparked fear in our hearts. The same silent question flitted through our minds: *Will there be more attacks?*

Sadness overwhelmed me as I realized the hopelessness of finding survivors in this gigantic funeral pyre. *What am I doing here at Ground Zero? How can I possibly help?*

These thoughts lasted a few seconds before conviction returned.

With my odd assortment of training, skills, and talents, this seemed the natural place for me to be. Sweeper Man, the first of many suffering persons who needed God's comfort, tore at my heart. Mourners cried over posted pictures of the missing. Workers and volunteers wore somber faces. People talked in hushed tones. Truly, this place was ripe for compassionate care and a resurgence of hope.

I know why I'm here; I can be nowhere else.

SECTION 2

Mission Almost Impossible

"We see our national character in rescuers working past exhaustion, in long lines of blood donors, in thousands of citizens who have asked to work and serve in any way possible. And we have seen our national character in eloquent acts of sacrifice. Inside the World Trade Center, one man who could have saved himself stayed until the end at the side of his quadriplegic friend. A beloved priest died giving the last rites to a firefighter. Two office workers, finding a disabled stranger, carried her down 68 floors to safety."

—President George W. Bush
Speech at National Cathedral
September 14, 2001

6

Heaven's Outpost in the Midst of Hell

"There is no exercise better for the heart than reaching down and lifting people up."

—John Holmes

In the blocks immediately surrounding the World Trade Center, one building stood unscathed: St. Paul's Chapel at 209 Broadway, thus earning its nickname "The Little Chapel That Stood."

On September 11, St. Paul's mission changed from ministering to its congregation to ministering to the weary and heartbroken. Located one block away from the carcasses of the Twin Towers, St. Paul's Chapel became 'home' to hundreds of volunteers and rescue and recovery workers.

Situated on the edge of hellish destruction, this refuge of rest and sanity served as heaven's outpost. The radical hospitality in this chapel of hope answered my prayers for shelter and food.

Completed in 1766, the oldest surviving church building in New York City had seen its share of history. George Washington's inauguration took place at St. Paul's on April 20, 1789. A specially marked pew bears his name where Washington worshipped. The chapel survived a major fire during the American Revolution that destroyed one-third of New York City.

And on September 11, "The Little Chapel That Stood" survived a terrorist attack, and withstood the gale-force discharge from the towers' collapse. Concrete, steel, asbestos, and glass shards stormed out of the sky. Computers and office equipment smashed to the pavement.

A blizzard of paper swirled around the church. A ghostly white ash mingled with cremated human dust blanketed St. Paul's historic cemetery. Despite its close proximity to Ground Zero, the Chapel received no damage: no shattered windows, no broken pillars, and no cracked roof tiles.

Four days after 9/11, St. Paul's opened a "Barbeque on Broadway" on the street outside the chapel. Over the next nine months of the rescue, recovery and clean-up operations, more than 5,000 volunteers joined together to serve more than a half-million meals during the chapel's operation as a care ministry.

However, initially, the Barbeque On Broadway ran into multiple tangles of red tape with the health and sanitation department, but received official approval to serve food on its premises. The food service moved indoors and became fully functional, complete with trained chefs. Donations poured in from benevolent persons to cover the cost of food, and restaurants donated meals.

The entire church staff carried out their jobs with quiet dignity. They never looked for favors or attention. The staff always aided physical needs, while looking out for our emotional and spiritual needs as well. I find it hard to single out any one member of St. Paul's staff for special attention because so many worked to help and comfort volunteers.

People gravitated to Reverend Lyndon Harris, Associate for Ministry at St. Paul's, who headed the team. A tender, strong man with a disarming smile, he was a true servant to everyone who passed through the chapel. I enjoyed talking to him and often observed him as he ministered to individuals and performed religious services in the chapel.

An energetic and efficient St. Paul's staff member, who stayed constantly on the phone, Katherine Avery worked out logistical issues and answered questions. Casually dressed in jeans, an oversized-denim shirt, and topped off with a NYPD cap, she handled the intake of donations like an air traffic controller, managing every donation flying in and out of St. Paul's airspace.

I met other St. Paul's staff members: Courtney Cowart, Martin Cowart (food captain at St Paul's), Rev. Dr. Frederic B. Burnham, and many others who worked behind the scenes to keep this sanctuary running smoothly.

But a thirty-something woman wearing a long-sleeved, gray habit stands out in my mind as the one who contributed the most to my stay at St. Paul's: Sister Grace of the Sisters of St. Margaret. From the first day I walked through the door at St. Paul's until the day I left, Sister Grace played a prominent role in my ministry at Ground Zero.

Sister Grace coordinated the chaplains' efforts. She possessed a special presence about her. Always polite and amicable, she looked out for the needs others, offering kind words of encouragement for everyone. An encourager and selfless caregiver with an ever-present, thin-lipped smile on her face, she kept tabs on me, and many others, through her litany of questions:

"How are you holding up?"

"Are you doing okay?"

"Do you need anything?"

"Are you getting some rest?"

"Did you eat dinner tonight?"

"Are you drinking enough water?"

Our Mother Hen hovered like a nurse assisting a doctor, anticipating our needs, checking on our welfare, and giving out big doses of encouragement. I loved working with Sister Grace, our lady of encouragement. She frequently handed me compassionate notes, cards, and letters written by people from around our country and the world to share with workers on the perimeter and on the Pile. Workers read these thoughtful writings on their short breaks, and the sentiments and support expressed in them often brought tears to their eyes.

Donations flooded into St. Paul's Chapel every day. Sister Grace often asked me and other chaplains to spread the caring expressed through this vast array of goodies. At various times we received and distributed crystal and plastic rosaries, figurines, Christmas ornaments, brand new wallets in original packaging, small make-up kits, money clips, tie clips with fire hydrants, tie clips with mini-handcuffs, small stuffed animals, and pocket toys. You name it, someone donated it. One southern volunteer claimed a cowboy belt buckle with a horse and "Hee-Haw" engraved on it.

I walked around the Pile with my turnout gear pockets stuffed with these odds and ends. When I stopped to chat with people, I pulled handfuls of these donations out of my pockets and asked, "Anyone want this stuff?"

These conversation starters often led to chats about families, personal matters, and sometimes, spiritual matters. Just as Sister Grace's love and encouragement was a gift to everyone who met her, the random gifts sent by fellow Americans encouraged the workers as they faced grueling conditions.

These trinkets—simple gestures of caring by strangers, tangible expressions of God's radical love—elicited unexpected smiles from faces drawn grim by their hellish, macabre tasks. God's grace transformed bits and pieces of curiosities into tangible gifts of love, kindness, and encouragement to the weary and heartbroken.

7

Ground Zero Crosses

"Any discussion of how pain and suffering fit into God's scheme ultimately leads back to the cross."

—Philip Yancey

O ur finite minds cannot begin to comprehend how God works in mysterious ways to care for His world and universe. But once in a while, God blesses humans with first-hand experience in how He accomplishes His purposes to make His presence known. I accepted God's answers to prayer: yes, no, or wait. Even a delay was an answer. However, my prayers related to the efforts at Ground Zero? Answers arrived quickly: "Yes."

One day Sister Grace approached me carrying a shoebox in her hands. "Here are some small wooden crosses. A woman from New Jersey makes them as her personal ministry. Pass them out to people on the perimeter and on the Pile. And here's a phone number to call when you need more." And as the loaves and fishes multiplied in the Bible, these crosses multiplied when we needed them.

Loving hands sanded and smoothed these beautiful crosses. I called them Ground Zero crosses and handed them out at every opportunity. A dove stamped on each cross reflected the peace, love, and hope God sends to His people. Each cross, with a bright-colored neck cord, was packed in a sandwich bag. Accompanying the cross, a small card shared this Bible verse: *"For God so loved the world that He gave His only begotten Son, that whoever believes in Him shall not perish, but have eternal life."* (John 3:16)

I met people on the perimeter and spent time listening to their stories and sorrows about their family members or friends lost on 9/11. When the opportunity arose, and when people asked spiritual questions, I offered them a cross. Everyone gladly accepted one and expressed gratitude to the woman who made them.

After a while, word spread, and people sought me out and requested crosses. The first box of crosses went fast, and I soon called my New Jersey cross maker to ask for more.

"These crosses are not good luck charms," I explained as I dispersed them. "They represent the work Jesus Christ did on the cross." These crosses touched people's hearts in their tender and most vulnerable moments, reminding them that God was near, and that He loved them in all of these trials and sufferings.

These crosses sometimes unlocked the floodgates of emotion, providing an opening to offer God's comfort. Men and women who were lonesome, afraid, overwhelmed, or deeply distressed asked for the crosses and for prayer. There was no shame in displaying these emotions in a place like this.

I sometimes felt lonesome myself—even a little afraid at times. But on those occasions, I joined with other chaplains or workers and shared some tears as we prayed and sang or talked about our families back home. That always made us feel better.

Each time I ran out of crosses, I called and asked the woman from New Jersey for more, and soon they arrived, stamped with their little symbols of peace, love, and hope.

8

Ground Zero Heroes

"Heroes may not be braver than anyone else. They're just braver five minutes longer."

—Ronald Reagan

First responders, the emergency workers, the firefighters, the police officers, the construction workers, the search and rescue teams, the search and recovery teams, and all the volunteers associated with the war-zone clean-up of ruin and loss—these were the true Ground Zero heroes. Showing strength deep within their souls, these men and women embodied the definition of endurance, heart, and true grit.

A hero willingly and knowingly risks personal safety and well-being for another human being. At Ground Zero, heroes of all kinds surrounded us: Military personnel at the perimeter helped us feel safe. The police patrolled and watched out for us. Firefighters and paramedics covered the city while recovery workers toiled on the Pile. Volunteers served the workers, and chaplains ministered to those in need.

These heroes worked long hours during the day and then worked more hours at night under blazing lights. Committed to teamwork, they worked to the point of exhaustion and beyond, single-minded in purpose and laser-focused on the job at hand. After the hope to find survivors faded, they doggedly searched for remains of friends and civilians.

Danger surrounded them. Cave-ins on the Pile occurred without warning. The air they breathed contained not only the stench of death, but also asbestos particles, fiberglass splinters, glass fibers, toxic chemicals, and incinerated human remains—air that could poison their futures. They sacrificed time with their families to serve their crews, their city, and their country.

Quiet and unassuming, the word "quit" did not exist in the Ground Zero heroes' vocabulary. They measured time not in billable hours, but in how well they accomplished each job.

Adapt.

Overcome.

Persevere.

Those words empowered them. Some didn't like the label "hero." Many brushed it off, insisting, "I'm just doing my job," or "I'm too busy to think of that nonsense." In a place where others lost their lives, some refused to be called heroes

A few said, "It's hard to be called a hero when you feel so beaten down and demoralized." But these folks rose out of the ashes and served well. They deserved to be called heroes.

We chaplains trod a delicate line to determine if our heroes needed support with their emotions. "How are you holding up?" we asked.

Sometimes we received gruff responses: "I'm fine. I don't need any help."

But at times, caring coworkers alerted us to those who worked on the Pile for days, refusing to go home or to shelters for food and rest. These folks dug deep within their souls to work those long hours. Such dedication and commitment. Even so, exhaustion started a downward spiral of mental and emotional exhaustion. We chaplains did what we could to help alleviate some of their suffering.

9

Serving on the Perimeter and the Pile

"Be kind, for everyone you meet is fighting a hard battle."

—Plato

My footprints covered the perimeter surrounding the 16-acre mountain of debris, leaving a lasting heart print on me and the volunteers who walked alongside me. Walking the circumference became a special ministry as we served the soldiers at the guard stations, the recovery workers on the Pile, the families and friends of those who lost their lives, plus the large numbers of concerned visitors who sojourned to the perimeter to pay their respects.

Many a day, I began walking the perimeter early in the morning, and in no time, morning melded into night. Where did the time go? Night dissolved into morning on the night shift, too, especially if we anticipated a body recovery. Sometimes, recovery personnel spotted remains down through gaps in the rubble, but the complexities of dealing with the unstable debris field and the intricate interconnections of steel and concrete meant recovery sometimes took hours. Adrenalin flowed in anticipation. Often we expected to retrieve remains at any minute, only to hear, "No, not yet. Wait. Soon, possibly." Removing major structural beams too quickly risked cave-ins or rubble slides. The shifting of the layers of metal and concrete caused constant delays, making time stand still for those waiting to assist. Recovery workers tunneled into the massive debris pile at great risk to their lives. Search and rescue dogs joined the efforts in the rubble heaps to find remains.

Recovery workers often didn't stop to take time to eat hot meals, even though the Salvation Army, nearby hotels, and the St. Paul's buffet on the terrace provided food around the clock. Volunteers from the food prep areas showed up at the perimeter and called to workers, "Hey, come and eat." But workers frequently lost all track of time and forgot about eating. When they ate, grit garnished their main course; the stench of the Pile remained in their noses. With blunted appetites, people ate out of necessity, not enjoyment.

When workers missed meals, chaplains and volunteers carried out God's plan by carrying food to them. We ported ice-cold water, sodas, Gatorade, sandwiches, chips, granola bars, and other treats in our ice chests and carry boxes. Workers who skipped meals welcomed our little brigade. They took short breaks and ate the food we provided, grit and all, then headed right back to work. Dirty hands were the least of their health risks at this point.

One time, I noticed a firefighter alone on the Pile. "Where's your crew?"

Seeing our food boxes he said, "They just took a short break, but they didn't get a chance to eat, and they're hungry."

"How many workers do you have in your unit?"

His answer did not surprise me. Like the multiplication of the loaves and fishes in the Bible, we 'just happened' to be carrying the exact number of meals needed for his whole crew.

Watching the workers was the hardest part of being around Ground Zero. Seeing them suffer from aching muscles, throbbing feet, parched mouths, gritty eyes, and sheer exhaustion hurt us, too. Despite their personal physical discomfort, they doggedly searched for remains of victims in the endless rubble.

One thing always cheered up Pile workers and guards: letters, cards, and drawings sent from schoolchildren and families. Our little brigade passed out this special mail and watched soldiers, policemen, and volunteers' faces light up as they read the caring messages.

Letters filled with encouraging words from adults delighted the workers, but children's notes touched their hearts and brought tears to their eyes. People around the country and around the world sent their love and hope in envelopes, and this support helped everyone press on through the tough days and nights.

Thank you, all of you, for your kindness and caring. God bless you. Never underestimate how a small gesture can encourage someone who's exhausted, sick, or despondent.

SECTION 3

Ministering in the Mess

"In prayer it is better to have a heart without words than words without a heart."

—John Bunyan

1 0

Prayer-walking the Perimeter

"Prayer is where the action is."

—John Wesley

With my tag-along group of volunteers, I "prayer-walked" the perimeter of Ground Zero on a regular basis. We went to each guard entrance around Ground Zero and offered to pray with the soldiers on duty. These guards protected us, and we wanted to show that God offered protection for them, too.

The first few times we did this, reception was slow. As time went by, the guards spotted me and my little troop of volunteers from St. Paul's headed their way and quickly huddled together for prayer.

Our prayers offering encouragement took only a few minutes. We always prayed for safety for them and their families. If a guard shared a particular worry, we included their concern in our prayers.

I prayed: "Father God, we pray for the safety of these workers as they go about taking care of their responsibilities, and we pray for their families. Give them gentle and soothing comfort. Place Your protective shield around them and keep them safe from harm. Amen."

On rare occasions, a few workers and guards didn't want to pray. We never forced the issue. I quietly lifted them up in prayer anyway while walking to the next guard station.

Eventually, some of the guards or workers wanted to take a turn to pray, too. Their purposeful, heartfelt prayers and caring words touched my heart. I listened, humbled by their beautiful tones and their tender concern for others. I loved hearing the prayers for their families and each other's safety as they stood their watch. That's how prayer is supposed to be.

Simple.

Clear.

From the heart.

This special prayer-walk time touched many people's hearts. We'd gather in a circle and hold hands or spread our arms around each other as we prayed. Occasionally, a person told me they felt spiritual comfort from our prayer time. I tried not to miss the prayer-walks around the perimeter, but once in a while, other duties on the Pile or counseling someone at St. Paul's Chapel kept me from doing the rounds.

On one occasion, I was astounded when someone asked for me specifically. The team waited for me to come and pray. Appreciation of the time we shared together encouraged me.

When we were busy on the Pile with mini-memorial services for exhumed pieces of humanity, we prayer-walked the perimeter later than usual. Even though we'd already worked long hours, we prayer-walked

because we noticed how important it was for the workers and also ourselves.

Prayer calmed the soul, starting us on a new track. Short, easy to memorize verses, like Psalm 27:3, encouraged the guards stationed around the perimeter and reminded me, *"Though a host encamp against me, my heart will not fear . . ."*

I used Psalm 3:1-4 often and ended up writing the Bible reference down for many to look up later. The biblical character David faced many dangers in his life. At one point, his son, Absalom, pursued him with the intent to murder him. But David turned to God in prayer, which we can use in our prayers. *"O Lord, how my adversaries have increased! Many are rising up against me. Many are saying of my soul, 'There is no deliverance for him in God.' But You, O Lord, are a shield about me, My glory, and the One who lifts my head. I was crying to the Lord with my voice, and He answered me from His holy mountain."*

I used words of Scripture as I prayed for the workers: *Lord, place Your protective shield around these workers. Keep their hearts free of anger and full of hope. Keep them safe from harm so they can return to their families. Thank You for Your promises in Scripture. We know You send answers to us from Your holy hill. Thank You for Your faithfulness to us, Lord. Amen.*

11

Fadda, Fadda, Can We Talk?

"There is no greater agony than bearing an untold story inside you."

—Maya Angelou

After September 11th, the common denominator of human suffering bonded everyone together in New York City. We all struggled, from street sweeper to firefighter at Ground Zero, from volunteer to high-ranking official, from office worker to family member, from church secretary to chaplains.

No one escaped the emotional agony accompanying this attack on New York City and our country. Everyone had a story: where he or she was when the terrorist attack occurred, which family member or friend was killed, who'd miraculously survived. Despite emotional pain almost beyond comfort, we also witnessed each other's inner strength.

In the early days after the attack, we couldn't say, "Time will heal this sorrow." The shock and devastation froze all comprehension of how one could ever possibly recover from such a life-shattering event. Even now, years later, we cry at annual memorial ceremonies when speakers stir our memories, reawakening feelings and anxieties about the terror attacks. Each new terror attack anywhere in the world triggers anxiety. However, the comfort we found in each other and in God helped us take each difficult, tiny step to move through the long journey of mourning.

At Ground Zero, people needed to talk about their experiences. Putting their stories into words was the first step to process their grief, even when the storytellers were unaware of this. Those who vented their sorrow experienced a measure of relief, but only for a time.

Haunting memories refused to leave. Flashbacks and nightmares revived fears. Telling and retelling these stories became a necessity. Non-talkers harbored their hurt and suffered silently, often alone, and probably for longer periods of time.

One day on the perimeter, while talking with another volunteer, a young NYPD officer tugged on my sleeve and interrupted our conversation.

"Fadda, Fadda," he said in a strong New York accent. "Can we talk, Fadda?" Clergy denominations like "Father" or "Reverend" or "Rabbi" didn't matter at Ground Zero. People saw our white clergy collars or CHAPLAIN written on our turnout gear and hard hats, and we became their spiritual fathers.

"Of course we can talk."

The NYPD officer's eyes flooded with tears. Trying to maintain his composure, his voice trembled as he spoke. "I'm supposed to be brave, but I'm scared. I saw that second airplane hit Tower 2, and I kept looking and looking. I couldn't turn away from that sight. I saw people in those windows with no hope . . . with smoke pouring out around them. No one could possibly reach them. And those jumpers . . . took my breath away. I saw ash-covered office workers and executives carrying brief cases running from that boiling, massive smoke-and-ash cloud charging down the street. So many people needed help, but I couldn't help anyone. I needed to run myself, but I froze on the spot."

He started to cry. "I thought, maybe this was it. Maybe my time had come. What could I do? Maybe there'd be another attack. Maybe I'd die."

I listened as this police officer rambled on until he talked through his emotional panic and calmed down a bit. I had no direct answers for him; he entertained the same questions we all asked. But one thing calmed my nerves—my faith in God and my hope in eternity.

After we talked for a while, the officer asked, "Can you pray for me?"

Like others and myself during times of deep fear and trembling, he appeared headed for a nervous breakdown. I shared Scripture offering these words of comfort for that dangerous emotional zone: *"[God] Himself has said, 'I will never desert you, nor will I ever forsake you,' so that we confidently say, 'The Lord is my helper, I will not be afraid. What will man do to me?'"* (Hebrews 13:5b-6)

As a man of faith himself, these particular verses comforted the officer. I often think of him and wonder how he's doing.

The pain, suffering, and tears I saw in this officer and many others brought me to my knees every day. As I talked with each person in distress, I waited through their panic attacks and listened through the rash of jumbled words until they calmed down. In this state of emotion, people just needed to talk. At this stage of the crisis, I was present, offered comfort, and shared a brief prayer, if wanted. I did not offer advice. I was just there to listen.

The physical and emotional obstacles those folks faced while working on the Pile evoked intense frustration and sorrow. God, prayer, and our friendship with each other helped us through. We could not have done it alone. We leaned upon the strength of our faith and verses like Psalm 34:17: *"The righteous cry, and the LORD hears and delivers them out of all their troubles."*

Emotional turmoil at Ground Zero was inescapable. We all suffered from anxiety and depression from time to time. When physical and emotional exhaustion controlled my body and brain, I escaped my darkest moments by picking up my Bible and reading about David's suffering in the Psalms.

His words resonated with my deflated feelings. Psalm after psalm, story after story, verse after verse portrayed David's agony and sorrowful pleadings to God, giving voice to my misery. I prayed David's words. *"Answer me when I call, O God of my righteousness!"* (Psalm 4:1) *"Give ear to my words, O LORD, Consider my groaning. Heed the sound of my cry for help."* (Psalm 5:1-2) *"Why do You stand afar off, O LORD?"* (Psalm 10:1) *"How long, O LORD? Will You forget me forever?"* (Psalm 13:1) *"Hear a just cause, O LORD, give heed to my cry."* (Psalm 17:1)

Throughout the 150 chapters of Psalms, David and other psalmists poured out their hearts to the Lord. Yet their pleadings always began or ended with praise for our all-powerful, all-knowing, all-present God, reminding me to praise God regardless of the circumstances.

"O LORD, our Lord, how majestic is Your name in all the earth." (Psalm 8:1) *"I will give thanks to the LORD with all my heart. I will tell of all Your wonders."* (Psalm 9:1) *"God is our refuge and strength, a very present help in trouble."* (Psalm 46:1) *"Great is the LORD, and greatly to be praised..."* (Psalm 48:1)

12

Bible Verse of the Day

"Just as love to God begins with listening to His Word, so the begin-ning of love for the brethren is learning to listen to them. It is God's love for us that He not only gives us His Word but also lends us His ear."

—Dietrich Bonhoeffer

Tucked in the left hip pocket of my firefighter's turnout coat, I carried my ever-present Bible. Everywhere I went at Ground Zero its black leather edges stuck out above my pocket visible to everyone. Its bulk weighed me down a bit as I ministered in the rubble, but I never left home without it.

Oh, hard-hatted, muscle-bound brutes on the Pile teased me for keep-ing my Bible handy, but I never wanted to quote God's Word without showing where the words came from. Those work-hardened heroes sometimes

expressed surprise when I recited Bible verses as answers to their questions.

"That's in the Bible?" they'd say. I pulled out my Bible from my side pocket and showed them.

I loved hearing, "Yo, Chaplain Bob. What's the verse for today?" on my prayer-walks around the perimeter at Ground Zero.

That question challenged me to find an uplifting verse to share each day. I didn't force Scripture passages on people, but offered to share scriptural encouragement with them when appropriate. People started asking for more Bible verses. Carrying a verse around in my heart each day not only kept my emotional balance, but encouraged others as well.

I didn't want to sound like I read these verses off a piece of paper or just made them up as I went along. Instead, I'd open the Bible and show where each verse was found.

The book of Proverbs provided many useful verses for my peripatetic trips around the perimeter and on the Pile. *"The proverbs of Solomon the son of David, king of Israel: To know wisdom and instruction, to discern the sayings of understanding, to receive instruction in wise behavior, righteousness, justice and equity . . . The fear of the Lord is the beginning of knowledge . . ."* (Proverbs 1:1-3)

At times, workers expressed anger on the Pile at the terrorists' actions. I hardly blamed them. The desire for revenge was a normal reaction to such tragedy and I shared some verses on this topic. I asked, "Can you imagine how the Lord will deal with these terrorists? Listen to Scripture's command. *"Never take your own revenge, beloved, but leave room for the wrath of God, for it is written, 'Vengeance is Mine, I will repay,' says the Lord... Do not be overcome by evil, but overcome evil with good.'"* (Romans 12:19, 21)

The revenge may not take place today or tomorrow or soon enough for us, or even in our lifetimes, but those strong words of promise reassure us that God has His plans firmly in hand. In other verses, God promises to be with us and to protect us: *"The Lord is for me; I will not fear; What can man do to me?"* (Psalm 118:6)

13

The Girl Who Was Crushed in Spirit

"We are each of us angels with only one wing, and we can only fly by embracing one another."

—Luciano de Crescenzo

While getting ready to do my prayer-walk on the perimeter one day, Sister Grace handed me an expensive little crystal angel with gold-trimmed wings. "Someone on the perimeter needs this guardian angel," she said. "Go find that person."

I tucked the three-inch tall angel in my pocket for safekeeping and decided to let the Holy Spirit guide me to the person who needed this blessing. I started my prayer-walk around the perimeter, stopping at each guard post to visit with my new friends. The National Guards and other workers in each area gathered in a circle for a quick prayer per our usual routine. At one station, a young female guard dressed in military fatigues and work boots stood back from the group, not wanting anything to do with God or prayer or chaplains.

I called over to her. "Would you like to join us in a brief prayer?"

"No," she said, voice terse.

"Okay, but we'll send a blessing your way anyway."

After we prayed, another soldier pulled me aside to tell me about the female guard. "She's having a difficult time with the gruesomeness of the recoveries on the Pile. She's gotten physically sick at the sight of the buckets of partial human remains."

I noticed her pain, but didn't want to push my God of comfort on her. I respected her privacy and personal choices. If someone asked about God or prayer or religion, then we chaplains willingly shared. I followed that strict rule to the letter.

But more often than not, workers and visitors to Ground Zero actually asked about God or asked for prayer. As I tried to express meaningful, yet succinct, answers about my faith, answering their probing questions about God refined my ministry skill.

As I watched this young woman, I thought she might be the perfect person for the crystal angel. I planned to give the figurine to her at my next opportunity. Over the next few days, I prayed privately for her quite a bit.

On another perimeter walk, I spotted her again. As I approached her guard post, other guards circled up for a brief prayer. Again she stayed off to the side.

Before joining the circle, I made my way over to her. "I have a little guardian angel for you if you'd like to have it, but I don't want to push it on you. I want to respect your feelings and privacy."

She looked down at the angel in my hand. After a few seconds, she said, "I'd like to have it."

I handed the crystal angel to her. Her hand wrapped around the translucent treasure, and then she placed her arms around my waist, leaned her head on my chest, and wept. The whole group of guards crowded around us and joined us in a group hug. Tears streamed down our faces.

With raw emotion and shaky voices, I thanked God for the blessings of that moment and offered a special prayer for comfort for this young woman. "Lord, I ask You to place an angelic hedge around this young guard. Keep her in Your watchful care and keep her mind and heart safe from despair. Bless her in this difficult work. Amen."

On each subsequent visit to this guard post, the young woman joined us in prayer and appeared to gain a measure of emotional strength.

All these hurting people and their stories had a therapeutic effect on me too. Even though I often joined them in their tears, focusing on their needs kept me from being an emotional mess myself. I felt honored and blessed to be associated with such courageous military and civilian men and women.

14

The Girl Who Needed Boots

"When I pray, coincidences happen, and when I don't, they don't."

—William Temple

One night, as I prepared to head out on my prayer-walk, Sister Grace handed me a brand new pair of heavy-duty, leather, steel-toed "Avenger" work boots to give to someone who needed them.

Sure, I thought, *no problem.*

Because of the brutal conditions on the Pile, the workers wore out foot gear left and right. But, oh. *These boots are small. Size 6. Who can possibly wear them?* Most hulking firefighters' feet, like mine, demanded size 13 or bigger.

I tied the corded shoelaces together and slung the boots around my neck like ice skates. I wore them that way for hours, asking people along my way, "Do you need a pair of size-sixers?"

That got lots of laughs and smart aleck comments from those big-hooved heroes. I prayer-walked the perimeter most of the night with that footgear hanging around my neck, praying for the person who needed them. As I stopped and chatted with each National Guard member stationed on the perimeter, I displayed these rough-and-ready Avengers, but not one person relieved me of my burden.

In fact, they rather enjoyed kidding me about them. The shoelaces burned red friction lines into my neck so I finally stowed the boots in my carry box.

Exhausted and ready to return to St. Paul's Chapel, I desperately needed sleep, but we still had to finish our prayer-walk around the perimeter. Besides, I didn't dare take my stringed albatross back to Sister Grace. Someone needed them.

Near the end of the prayer-walk, just before heading back to St. Paul's, we stopped at one last guard station. I told the guards there about the work boots in my carry box.

A young female National Guardsman spoke up, ecstatic. She showed me her badly damaged boots, and said, "Look at these boots. They're ruined, and I can't afford to buy new boots."

I pulled out the size-6 boots and held them out to her. She tried them on and grinned—a perfect fit. Her delight was classic—a perfect Cinderella story. Better yet, a perfect God-answers-prayer story. And, oh, I looked forward to seeing Sister Grace's delight, even though she wouldn't be surprised at all. Sister Grace understood how God worked behind the scenes on our behalf.

SECTION 4

The World's Biggest Crime Scene

"The only reason I got called a hero is because I got caught doing what so many others did as well. There were over three thousand lives needlessly taken from us on 9/11. But you must remember that there were also over one hundred thousand acts—99 percent of them anonymous and undocumented—of comfort and aid and bravery and sacrifice and kindness that day. These people were all heroes."

—Michael Benfante, *Reluctant Hero*

15

Rescue and Recovery

"The noir hero is a knight in blood-caked armor. He's dirty and he does his best to deny the fact that he's a hero the whole time."

—Frank Miller

In the massive morgue of debris at Ground Zero, search and rescue workers initially found only a few survivors.

Within a week after 9/11, the focus of Ground Zero work changed from search and rescue to search and recovery of human remains. This gruesome task challenged the mental, emotional, and spiritual capacities of everyone involved.

I watched firsthand as our ground heroes searched for remains partially buried underneath a downed stories-tall structural beam. Searchers crawled into a ten-foot-deep crevice under the beam where the remains lay trapped, all the while worrying the beam might shift or debris slide down and crush them.

I wondered why they didn't just move the beam first, but a firefighter pointed out, "It's a vertical structural beam of enormous length, and it's interconnected with other steel beams."

I tried to follow the size of the beam with my eyes, but couldn't find the end. Debris piles hid large sections. Even after he explained it to me, I still couldn't figure out how this beam had been part of any building.

The whole Ground Zero debris Pile was like that for me. Since I was unfamiliar with original layout of the land before the attacks, what I saw made no sense. The first time I saw before and after pictures of the WTC site and where things stood originally, I was amazed.

Another day, I saw a firefighter's excitement when he found a friend's axe partially buried in the rubble. Firefighters take great pride in their equipment, knowing these tools can mean the difference between life and death. They inscribe their names on their tools and treat them with care. Finding this axe teased hopes of finding more of his buddy's remains.

Finding human remains was emotionally harder than finding firefighter tools. No one escaped the emotional pain triggered by these discoveries. One day, the recovery searchers discovered five or six pairs of firefighter boots with severed legs still in them. The rest of their bodies remained missing. I can't dwell on this description because my mind flashes right back to that scene, stirring intense feelings.

Trying to find fallen firefighters in the Ground Zero rubble was tough. The physical, mental, and emotional strain was hard on the surviving crews. I've never lost a close friend in a line of duty situation, but anytime a firefighter falls, they're still a brother. The pain from a loss was great. We saw the anguish on the faces of firefighters and police officers at funerals. Courageous men struggled through their honor guard duty with contorted faces, quivering lips, and tears. Grief pounded our hearts, taking us to our knees.

Another time, we found a human head—nothing else. We placed the head in a body bag. Sometimes we found hands. Sometimes we found fingers. Searchers recovered buckets of fingers and thumbs from the rubble. One group of searchers found two clasped hands, a man's and a woman's. These two tried to comfort each other in the midst of the terrible chaos of the attack. I shuddered as I pictured two jumpers holding hands as they leapt from Tower 1 to escape the smoke and flames.

I forgot my Hollywood-set mentality and let my guard down. I'd been to this area of the Pile many times before, but the reality of finding remains in these lower levels pummeled me again: over 2800 people were burned and crushed to death in this gargantuan crematorium. Thank God thousands escaped in that small window of time between the first attack and the collapse of the buildings. And thank God for those first responders who went into those burning buildings to escort people out.

How hard it must have been for all those Ground Zero heroes who not only knew the layout of the land, but recognized their buddies' remains and then held their torment in check upon discovering them.

Some tough guys professed, "Oh, I've handled bodies before. I can do this." Others took it hard.

So many mixed emotions churned through those searchers: piercing pain, overwhelming sorrow, tenacious frustration, and anger. Large numbers of human remains laid trapped all around us and beneath us. At night, under the blazing lights, the scene became even more surreal. All those shadowy caverns and chasms created by the collapsed, heat-damaged steel and crushed concrete held unknown terrors.

As we searched for human remains and meaning in the midst of suffering, it was daunting to think we worked in the middle of a mass-murder crime scene. I found myself in prayer many times pleading to God to protect us against damage to our minds, *Bless these workers, Lord. Protect their hearts and minds. Give them the ability to overcome their anguish. Keep them safe as they work. Amen.*

I have no regrets at showing my emotions. In *Man's Search for Meaning*, Viktor Frankl, the survivor of four Nazi concentration camps, eloquently expressed what volunteers and those working on the Pile demonstrated: "There was no need to be ashamed of tears, for tears bore witness that a man had the greatest of courage, the courage to suffer."

Many times, overcome with grief myself, I leaned on the men and women around me. The struggle all around me and within myself made me stronger, and also more tender.

16

I'm Sorry, Son

"For the dead and the living, we must bear witness."

—Elie Wiesel

A glint of reflected light from high up on the smoking Pile caught the fire chief's attention. For seconds, he stared through the hazy, dust-filled air toward a section of still-standing WTC façade some thirty feet away.

He bolted off toward the gleam, scrambling awkwardly over the unstable pile of hot twisted beams, bent rebar, and concrete chunks. Not caring for his personal safety, he darted across the wobbly, shifting surface of the debris.

As he reached the higher point on the Pile, he stopped and stood still. I caught up with him and saw what he'd spotted from a distance: a firefighter's Self Contained Breathing Apparatus (SCBA), its air bottle crushed and exploded, like a frozen aluminum soda that expanded and exploded. Now the SCBA lay smashed almost beyond recognition.

A dust and ash-coated piece of black turnout coat, so filthy it blended in with the surrounding grayish debris, lay next to the smashed SCBA. And then, we saw something more disheartening: the partially decomposed remains of a NYFD firefighter. The body looked like a large ball of mucousy dough coated and rolled in dirt. Grimy with ash, the slimy bundle was clearly a limbless, headless human torso. The scorching heat of burning fires below the surface of the Pile accelerated the decomposition process. The smell of putrefying flesh and the rotting of human remains gagged me. My stomach lurched and bile burned in my throat. I held my breath, inhaling only the shallowest sips of air. My eyes flooded with tears, my jaw ached with pain from gritting my teeth.

The strong, tough fire chief stared at the remains of his fallen firefighter, bowed his head in reverence, then choked out these soft-spoken words with the tenderness of a father mourning his only son. "I'm sorry, son. So, so sorry."

I touched the chief on the shoulder, and he turned and leaned in to me. We stood there side-by-side, arms around each other, holding each other tight, tears flowing. After a few minutes, I whispered a prayer of comfort in the chief's ear: "Lord, it's so hard for us to look at this firefighter. We feel such sorrow for his family members and fellow firefighters who anguish over this great loss. Knowing You will hold onto this firefighter for eternity, we pray that finding these remains will help bring a measure of comfort to his loved ones. Thank You, Lord, for helping us find this hero. Bring comfort to everyone here on this Pile who's witnessed this recovery. Restore their hope in a brighter future. Amen."

A team of recovery workers climbed up the rubble heap and joined us near the remains. They, too, fell silent. They tore off their safety helmets and masks as signs of respect for their fallen hero. Tears marked trails down their ash-covered faces, lips quivered with reined-in emotion, heads bowed, shoulders slumped.

After a few minutes, recovery workers retrieved the remains so the family had something to bury. They tenderly placed the firefighter's remains on a fluorescent orange plastic stretcher, and then covered him with an American flag.

Again, I offered a short prayer of comfort for the family of the fallen firefighter but also for the recovery workers and the other members of this firefighter's crew. I read Psalm 23, pausing to insert a few brief comments: "The Lord is our Shepherd who watches over us even in death and comforts us in eternity where we will meet again. Amen."

All work at the site stopped as the firefighters carried their brother off the Pile in an orderly procession. Loud construction noise ceased as heavy equipment, backhoes, front-end loaders, and 18-wheeler dump trucks stopped work. Grim-faced fellow workers formed lines, stood at attention, saluting as the somber parade passed them.

A firefighter who saved lives shouldn't be dead, but he was—his annihilation caused by terrorists who cared nothing about the sanctity of human life.

Questions swirled in our minds: *Why did these terrorists do such an evil thing? Where was God?*

Deeply saddened by this death, the firefighters, police officers, and recovery workers' determination remained strong. Americans can never forget this tragic scene, ever. These firefighters will not have died in vain if America always remembers their sacrifice on September 11, 2001.

17

Waiting for Recoveries

"We can be tired, weary and emotionally distraught, but after spend-
ing time alone with God, we find that He injects into our bodies
energy, power and strength."

—Charles Stanley

Slow and tedious recovery operations required meticulous care to move debris lest lower levels with caverns collapsed further. It was no easy task to move the tons of rebar and heavy steel beams, but it was almost poetic watching those experts operate the cranes and jaws to manipulate the steel beams and concrete chunks around. At times, the equipment operators made the process look easy. Their precise ma-neuvering looked like threading a needle with cranes, hooks, and clam shovels on their long arms.

Once we stood by for hours waiting for recovery workers to extract a Port Authority officer from the interlocked layers of building materials trapping his remains. Partially buried beneath building refuse, they spot-ted his mutilated remains down through a shaft in the debris.

Two young chaplains, recent arrivals at Ground Zero, waited with me, eager to help at the Pile. They hadn't yet seen impromptu mini-sermons and prayers conducted after recovery of remains and were a bit anxious about leading the service by themselves.

Over time, I officiated over 300 mini-memorials. I often used brief excerpts of Psalm 23 and generally made a few comments during those on-the-spot, Ground Zero mini-memorial services for fallen firefighters, police officers, and civilians. I went over the mini-memorial format a few times with the young chaplains, and they grasped what to say and how to handle the memorial service.

I was beyond exhaustion and these inexperienced chaplains felt confident to oversee the service. I left them and returned to the chapel to catch a few winks. Within a short time, someone woke me, "The two chaplains need you to come back to the Pile."

That power nap revived me a bit, and I went back to meet them. We conducted the memorial service together. We gathered all the workers who labored to recover this Port Authority officer and prayed for their well-being.

A time of deep reflection for us all, we chaplains stayed a little longer, sitting alongside the Pile on a steel beam amid the rubble, sharing our thoughts, praying, and singing old familiar hymns like "Blessed Assurance." Our solemn time together ended with us praising God for His greatness.

Blessed assurance, Jesus is mine!/Oh, what a foretaste of glory divine!
Heir of salvation, purchase of God,/Born of His Spirit, washed in His blood.
Refrain:
This is my story, this is my song,/Praising my Savior all the day long;
Perfect submission, perfect delight,/Visions of rapture now burst on my sight;
Angels, descending, bring from above/Echoes of mercy, whispers of love.
Perfect submission, all is at rest,/I in my Savior am happy and blest,
Watching and waiting, looking above,/Filled with His goodness, lost in His love.
This is my story, this is my song,/Praising my Savior all the day long.

Even in dismal circumstances, God's comfort surrounded us and His words from Hebrews 10:23 strengthened us: *"Let us hold fast the confession of our hope without wavering, for He who promised is faithful...."*

18

Follow the Flies

"Birds are the eyes of heaven, and flies are the spies of hell."

—Suzy Kassem

In a 7-story deep pile of construction debris, how do you begin to search for human remains? Sitting off to the side of the Pile one day, I watched as search and rescue teams scoured the debris looking for remains. At this point, for safety reasons, the authorities asked chaplains to stand aside and not assist in recoveries. One fire chief and I chatted away about my past experiences as a licensed funeral director and embalmer in the Chicago area. As we talked, we noticed swarms of flies concentrated in an area of the Pile.

"That might be a good place to search," I said. "Flies love dead flesh."

The fire chief turned and looked at me. "You've got to be kidding. Flies can help us?"

I nodded my head. "I'm not kidding."

He directed the crews to search in that area and soon after we found quite a bit of human tissue. "Follow the flies" soon became a common quote on the Pile.

We also used our senses to find bodies. Our sense of smell often led us to recoveries of remains. The stench of death, a distinctive, unmistakable odor, clung to our noses and clothes. Although at this point we

74

wore masks to protect us from the bad air and the noxious odors on the Pile, the smell of rotting flesh still assailed us. We constantly adjusted or tightened the straps to keep particulate in the air from filtering in the sides of the masks.

At times, we ripped the masks off our faces because of the discomfort. Sweat and mucous gathered around our mouths and noses and collected in our throats. A gritty, sand-like taste parched our mouths. Which was worse? The strong whiffs of decaying bodies with the masks off? Or the taste of the mucous collecting in our throats with the masks on?

My knowledge of anatomy helped on the Pile, too. As I finished conducting a mini-funeral, searchers uncovered more remains. One searcher brought a specimen over. "What's this?"

"Can I take a look at it?" He handed it to me. "This is a part of a pelvic bone with flesh and tailbone still attached."

"Now how would you know that?"

"I have degree in mortuary science and pathology."

He looked at me. "Are you serious?" Shaking his head, he returned to work.

Later in the day, another official-looking person from the morgue inquired about the same remains. "Who ID'd that sample?"

Uh, oh, I thought. *I'm in trouble.* I owned up to identifying the specimen while wondering, *How did I make a mistake?*

Instead, he nodded. "Thanks. It's nice to see human remains correctly marked. How did you identify the bone?"

"I was an x-ray tech in the military and later earned a mortuary science and pathology degree."

"Nice job. We appreciate your help."

Afterward, a different morgue technician approached me, "Would you help offsite with morgue work?"

"I'll help if you really get in a pinch, but my ministry here comes first to offer God's comfort and hope to the grieving families and workers."

The attack on 9/11 brought the plague of terrorism and suffering to our shores. From the roar of the jets slamming into the Twin Towers to the whirring of flies on the Pile, the grievous swarm of flies hovering near the dead provided just one more reminder of mass murderers enslaved by hard hearts who threw aside the value of the sacredness of life.

Just as swarms of flies covered Pharaoh's Egypt and attached themselves to men and beasts, horror covered our hearts as anguish adhered to our spirits. Just as flies feasted on human remains, spiritual havoc feasted on our faith. Just as many people wrestled with spiritual issues at Ground Zero, I shared my faith—even though that meant sharing in their sorrow and horror.

Many times around the perimeter of Ground Zero or at St. Paul's Chapel, exhausted and emotionally drained workers or volunteers noticed my Bible jutting out of my pocket. The pain and plague of terrorism ripped opened their hearts and probing questions spilled out. They asked about death, marriage, suffering, children, anger, revenge, heaven, and hell. Following Jude 1:22's counsel, *"And have mercy on some, who are doubting,"* I opened my Bible and flipped to scriptural answers to their challenges.

Over the years for quick reference, I highlighted many biblical passages underscoring God's numerous promises. At a glance, questioners observed colored markings on the pages of my open Bible. Praise for God, advice for living life, promises about the hope of eternity, insight about anger and revenge, and observations on hardships and trials glowed from my Bible.

19

Postcards from Hell?

"Life's never a postcard of life, is it? It never feels like how you'd want it to look."

—*Russell Brand*

One hot late-fall day, our small group of chaplains, sweaty and tired, stood chatting by the Pile. A firefighter working near us noticed something among the debris and called us over to look. At first, it was hard to tell what we were examining, but I soon guessed it was the remains of a woman's torso wearing a bluish blouse. Her decomposing body emanated an overpowering odor. Holding our breath as long as possible, we worked quickly to extricate her from the concrete chunks and tangled wires. At last, we lifted her remains from the rubble, tagged them for DNA purposes, and placed them in a body bag and on a stretcher.

I read a bit of Scripture, and we prayed the remains would be identified and the family notified for proper burial. After the stretcher carried her body away to the morgue, we continued searching for more remains. As we moved smaller pieces of debris, I found seven picture postcards so smelly, dirty, and crumpled that it was hard to identify the scenes on the cards. I wiped them off on my pants, then realized the cards were pictures of the Twin Towers standing majestically in the New York City skyline. The caption on the post cards said "On Top of the World." The possibility struck me. *These may have come from the gift shop on the 110th floor, the observation deck of Tower 2. The woman in the blue blouse might have been a gift shop employee.*

I imagined standing on the observation deck of this towering building and staring at a plane headed directly at her. *What thoughts coursed through the terror-stricken woman's head in the last minutes of her life? Did she survive the impact only to find herself trapped in a smoke-suffocating room? Did she immediately understand she had no chance of survival?*

One minute she was calmly arranging or looking at postcards in the gift store, and the next moment, her world ended. Thunderous, ear-spitting noise and deafening explosions. Walls caving in. Ceiling tiles collapsing. Glass display cases shattering. I prayed that only seconds passed before she mercifully lost consciousness.

One postcard showed exquisite fireworks against the New York City skyline. A tourist might have written "Wish you were here" or "Sending my love from the Top of the World." No messages to family members and friends or addresses were written on these cards.

Later I placed those postcards in plastic baggies to preserve them. When I speak to various groups, I display them alongside books, photos, and a few other Ground Zero artifacts. Awestruck by normal, everyday items, people imagine the horrors this woman experienced.

If someone had mailed those cards to a loved one before dying in the towers, would the receiver reread that postcard every day forever? When I'm away from my wife on occasion, and I receive letters or cards from her, I read her words many times a day. I carry her letters with me until they look shabby from so much handling. Those last letters and notes from those killed hold special meaning for loved ones.

We have a precious love letter from God—the Bible. The Bible, a story of redemption from Genesis to Revelation, reveals God's love for us. God's Son, Jesus, died for us and His love letter is our link to the reality of eternity with God.

When we face earthly suffering, God's message offers us hope. Our lives on earth are merely a speck in the sands of time, but our eternal life with God will continue on forever. We can claim these hope-filled promises from 2 Corinthians 4:16-18 in the Bible: *"Therefore we do not lose heart, but though our outer man is decaying, yet our inner man is being renewed day by day. For momentary, light affliction is producing for us an eternal weight of glory far beyond all comparison, while we look not at the things which are seen, but at the things which are not seen; for the things which are seen are temporal, but the things which are not seen are eternal."*

2 0

The President, The Mayor, The Governor, The Politician

"A politician thinks of the next election. A statesman, of the next generation."

—James Freeman Clark

In the first few weeks after the terrorist attacks, many local, state, national, and international dignitaries visited Ground Zero. They supported and encouraged families who lost loved ones and bolstered the spirits of the workers and volunteers enduring the hellish conditions.

On September 14, 2001, President Bush climbed on an ash-covered, charred fire truck atop the shifting pile and spoke through a bullhorn. "I want you all to know that America today is on bended knee in prayer for the people whose lives were lost here, for the workers who work here, for the families who mourn."

"We can't hear you," someone in the crowd yelled.

President Bush pulled the bullhorn closer to his mouth and said, "I can hear you! The rest of the world hears you! And the people—and the people who knocked these buildings down will hear all of us soon."

The crowd chanted *"U.S.A., U.S.A. U.S.A.,"* drowning out the president's words.

After a few minutes, the president continued, "The nation sends its love and compassion to everybody who's here. Thank you for your hard work. Thank you for making the nation proud, and may God bless America."

Later that day, speaking as the Commander-in-Chief and America's Chaplain, Bush added, "Grief and tragedy are only for a time. But goodness, remembrance, and love have no end. The Lord of life holds all who die, all who mourn."

Although not present in Manhattan when the president visited Ground Zero, I was on the Pile when the Mayor of New York City, Rudolph W. Giuliani, visited for a memorial service for all who lost their lives—police, firefighters, and civilians. Even though these were the worst of times for Mayor Rudolph Giuliani and his city, he provided strong leadership and had our best interests at heart. I retain good memories of his visit and his interactions with the hundreds of firefighters, police officers, emergency workers, construction workers, and volunteers who attended that memorial service.

This aggressive attack affected Mayor Giuliani both as the leader of the city and also personally. He lost close friends and work associates between the assaults on the WTC and the Pentagon in Washington, D.C. He attended over two hundred funeral services and wakes for firefighters and police officers who died in the collapsed towers. At one funeral, in his deep soothing voice, he assured the firefighter's children, "Know that your father is a hero. He lives inside you. And he always will."

On 9/11, trapped for a short time by smoke and ash in an office on Barclay Street, two blocks from the South Tower, Mayor Giuliani's security team led him to safety through a basement exit on Church Street. He ventured out onto the streets near the World Trade Center to view the events taking place. Covered in ash and sometimes putting on a mask, he spoke to media reporters as he walked, giving information and directions: "Evacuate all areas below Canal Street. To reach safety, walk north."

Online videos show Mayor Giuliani's first view of the burning, smoking towers including the sight of a person jumping from one of the highest floors of the tower. This image, he said, was permanently engraved in his memory. As Tower 2 collapsed, Giuliani and his entourage rushed toward the north to escape the toxic smoke and ash clouds billowing down the streets. As he sprinted to safety, he experienced the same breathlessness and panic as those around him.

On October 28, 2001, I met Mayor Giuliani who offered a comforting message to New Yorkers, the nation, and the world. After first sharing compassionate thoughts for those who lost their lives in the attack, he encouraged workers logging long hours on the Pile. Instead of bemoaning the past or expressing anger toward the terrorists who committed this heinous act, he pointed to the future with a positive message: "We will rebuild New York City, and we will be a stronger city as a result of this attack."

The crowd pressed in all around him. Everyone wanted a piece of him: a photo, a handshake, a question, a moment in time with him. The mayor, present for the memorial service, didn't necessarily want the attention, but he took time to greet people. I admit that I wanted my picture with him, too. And, yes, I got it. I did not mean to disrespect his purpose or presence on the Pile, but my selfish human nature took over.

I gave Mayor Giuliani a hug and thanked him for his courage and strength under the circumstances. I handed him a small wooden Ground Zero cross, the Christian symbol of the hope of eternity, and wished him well.

He said to me, "If you need anything, please ask." His leadership and compassion touched me.

As happens in the backwash of all major tragedies, Mayor Giuliani received praise as well as criticism for what he did or didn't do after 9/11. However, I witnessed his strength and stamina to lead his great city through a terrible time in its history.

I gained a new respect for this man. He showed fortitude by going into the crowd of workers, greeting people, shaking hands, and speaking with the men and women present. Although members of his security team remained close by, they did not prevent Mayor Giuliani from speaking to and inspiring his fellow New Yorkers.

Later, I briefly met the Governor of New York, George Pataki, as he toured the Pile. I gave him a small Ground Zero cross and thanked him for visiting the Pile and offering his encouragement and support.

By contrast, a few visitors to the Pile fell short of representing leadership or expressing compassion. One 'to-remain-nameless' famous politician emitted a cocky air of insincerity and "I'm here just for the political photo op." With his hands stuffed in his pockets, he refused to reach out and shake hands with anyone. His disappointing actions and body language failed to impress those of us working on the Pile.

These visiting politicians, though largely performing their civic duty, inspired all those involved in the work at Ground Zero, renewing their determination to keep going despite the miserable circumstances.

SECTION 5

The Heart of the Matter

"The rescue workers went through a hopeful stage, and then a disappointed one, and have all come to one of acceptance. Yet while everyone is making progress in that respect, I fear that most firefighters have not yet integrated the full horror of the situation into their day-to-day life in a way that will genuinely enable them to move forward."

—Dennis Smith, *Report from Ground Zero.*

21

Hard Shells, Soft Hearts

"An abnormal reaction to an abnormal situation is normal behavior."

—Viktor Frankl, *Man's Search for Meaning*

Every day at Ground Zero, we experienced emotional pain and discouragement along with anxiety and anger toward the sheer vastness of this mass murder crime scene and its perpetrators. Our inability to better manage our work and emotions frustrated us.

Recovery workers handled emotional pain in a wide variety of ways. Some who recovered human remains stood for long moments frozen in respectful, reverent silence. Seasoned firefighters saluted fallen buddies, as tears slipped down their faces. Unabashed, others wept and embraced each other. No one ever mocked others for crying, a normal response to the deaths of several thousand people.

Other stoic workers didn't pause in their work. They plugged away, moving beams, hauling trash, investigating crevices. Did they suspect if they stopped, they'd nosedive into an emotional heap? I don't understand how this last group managed to hold themselves together for so long. A matter of emotional survival, working was their way to respond to intense pain. For the most part, people on and around Ground Zero wanted to talk about what bothered them, about their memories, or about the difficult recovery they'd made. Talkers who wanted to share a burden sometimes sought out a chaplain.

While on the Pile I heard cussing and fussing and all kinds of foul or obscene language—a normal response to intense pain. Even though profanity offended me, I ignored my discomfort and stayed close by, ready to offer an ear for someone who needed to vent. Little things triggered these angry outbursts of cursing, opening up the emotional floodgates to liberate deeper pain. One guy whacked his hand moving heavy debris and discharged a wild string of obscenities. He turned, noticed me standing nearby and said, "Pardon my French, Father."

I smiled. "I don't remember those words in French class."

He laughed, breaking the tension. We both returned to work.

After a while, the mountain of debris grew smaller. Slowly but surely, things started looking better at the Pile. Workers rallied with new energy, refusing defeat despite the remaining months of backbreaking endeavors. As we conquered part of this tragedy's darkness, sometimes we heard laughter.

The ash and smoke-filled air started to clear. Families visited the Ground Zero viewing platform to conduct dedications and memorial services for lost loved ones and I smelled their flowers. At times, instead of death, I smelled food cooking at makeshift eating places. Now I tasted grit-free lasagna and savored the taste of the Coke I drank when parched.

Workers and volunteers shook hands and hugged in the joy of overcoming harsh tragedy. History proved once again: When a powerful blow knocks Americans to their knees, we pray, rise again, and go back to work—more powerful, resilient, and stronger than before.

22

The Cynic

"The greater part of the truth is always hidden, in regions out of the reach of cynicism."

—J. R. R. Tolkien

Working on the Pile brought out the best in people—but sometimes it provoked the worst.

Chaplaincy training taught that outbursts of anger and rage, fits of profanity, sarcastic and cynical comments, bouts of hysterical crying, or periods of muteness were normal reactions to abnormal situations. Polite people acted out with verbal harshness. Loud people withdrew into silence and despair. Timid people acted with bravery.

People react differently in traumatic situations, and no one response is better or worse than any other. People may remember and wish they hadn't spoken or acted in a certain manner, but in the heat of sorrow or the emotional drama of the moment, they remain incapable of making that judgment.

Chaplains, individually and as a group, sometimes became the target for emotional outbursts, just as caretakers absorb the brunt of inappropriate behavior from loved ones. One night, after spending eighteen hours on the Pile, I was so exhausted I couldn't walk straight. I felt heartsick for the recovery workers searching for remains of their buddies and other victims. These folks, brain drained and physically exhausted, continued to work. Their determination amazed me.

On a few earlier tours to Ground Zero, I'd overextended myself, but by now, I recognized my limitations: Physical exhaustion preceded emotional and mental exhaustion, and I realized I needed rest.

As I left the inner Pile and headed to St. Paul's Chapel for some food and rest, I met up with seven NYPD officers coming on duty. They looked at me, dirty-faced and covered in ash and sweat. One of them said, "Chaplain Bob, no offense, but you look like hell."

I believed it. I felt that way, too.

Then another officer asked, "Did you pray for anybody today? As if that would help."

Noting his sarcastic tone, but ignoring it, I smiled. "Yes, I prayed a lot out there on the Pile, and I do believe it helps. If nothing else, it keeps me sane, although some people around me might argue that point." I quickly changed the subject. "Are you guys starting your shift?"

"Yes," one replied.

"May I pray for you before you go on duty?"

They agreed, but the one who'd scoffed about prayer hesitated.

I said to him, "It's okay. You can stand in or out, but I'm going to pray for all you brave men and your families, including you, officer."

The other officers circled up, arms over shoulders, ready for a prayer. The angry officer didn't immediately respond to the invitation to join the prayer circle.

However, he stepped into the circle with his work buddies and bowed his head after I began to pray. "Thank You, God, for the courage of these fine men who protect us all by working in this horrible place and time in history. The bravery of these fine officers surpasses any courage I've seen or ever been associated with until now. Thank You, God, for these officers who watch our backs on the perimeter to keep us from worrying about our immediate safety. Please provide guardians to watch over and protect their families and the people they dearly love. Keep them alert and strong as they work. Thank You, God, for all of our protectors this evening. Amen."

I shook each man's hand and thanked him for his service, then headed back to St. Paul's Chapel. One officer caught up to me and hugged me. He started to tear up as he apologized for his crew member's behavior. He added, "I've never heard prayer like that before."

"You'd be amazed at what the Holy Spirit can do in your life through prayer," I replied.

After that, this police officer joined me in prayer a few more times. I still remember him and his buddies and send a prayer their way, every now and then.

23

The Mocker

"Don't let your fear of being judged stop you from asking for help when you need it."

—Author Unknown

During my time at the Pile, I approached individuals working and typically asked, "How are you holding up?"

The most common reply I received was: "I'm okay. I don't need a chaplain, but thanks for checking on me." Even so, I still stuck around silently and observed.

Similar to the stigma of talking to a psychiatrist, I realized the potential embarrassment that might coincide with talking with a chaplain.

"Others might think I'm weak or mentally fragile."

"Oh, he must be nuts."

"He's losing his grip on reality."

"He's having a tough time emotionally."

Or, heaven forbid, "He's too soft." And "He's losing his crackers."

As a chaplain, I worked through that same litany in my mind when another person or chaplain inquired, "How are you doing?"

My polite reply? "I'm okay. Thanks for asking."

But, truth of the matter? I hurt badly from sleep deprivation and physical exhaustion. As I observed the humanity and broken-heartedness of the men and women on the Pile, I became more and more emotional and tenderhearted. From street sweepers to the highest-ranking officials, we all tried to bury our emotions on the inside to be strong for others. Nobody wanted the label "weakling" or "crybaby," even those of us who knew better.

One day as the machines lifted beams and rebar in a potential recovery spot, I waited on the sidelines of the Pile with a bunch of firefighters. Joking with one another was usually a good sign you're among friends and you've built a trusting relationship. I sometimes got teased about being a "Preacher" or a "Bible Thumper." These names were generally said in good-humored fun, as a way to pass some time, and I never took offense. However one day, one person went above and beyond normal teasing.

"We don't need any Jesus people here. I don't want to hear your Bible thumping. We all have our beliefs and don't want to hear yours. None of the guys here need you. We're fine. So why don't you just excuse yourself and wander off and be a goody-two-shoes somewhere else?"

Whoa. That was quite a barrage. Where did it come from? What was behind his diatribe? I was just sitting and chewing the fat with the guys, and not preaching or Bible banging at all. That's not my style.

Feeling awkward, I stood up. "Okay, fellas, if you need me, you know where you can find me." Then I politely excused myself.

As I walked a little way from the group, one firefighter caught up to me and said, "Hey, Chaplain. This guy doesn't speak for everyone in the group. He's just a changed man through all of this. He used to be a fun-loving regular guy, but now he's angry and in deep pain. He lost close buddies, and that's affected his whole attitude."

Chaplaincy work requires a thick skin. I perceived that the officer who unloaded on me carried some heavy emotional burdens. While I didn't take offense at his sarcastic comments, still his verbal abuse stung my heart. When doing your best to help in a horrific situation, it's considerate to receive appreciation rather than criticism. I thanked the young man for his information and left him with a prayer.

Later that evening at St. Paul's Chapel, I looked up to see the young firefighter who'd scorned me earlier. "Can we talk?" he asked.

I patted the chair beside me. "Of course."

Already physically exhausted and emotionally drained, I didn't want another negative interaction with further verbal insult. But this time the young man didn't have an audience, and he aired a different, more vulnerable attitude.

He apologized for his angry outburst and his unfair treatment of me in front of his comrades. With tear-filled eyes and anguished sighs, he related story after story about his fallen buddies. As he shared his pain, our hearts connected and salty kinship spilled from my eyes.

When I look back on these different stories and realize the depth of human pain and suffering triggered by 9/11, I'm humbled before God. How does He hold up and deal with all this tragedy and prayer we send His way?

24

Loving Others—No Matter What

"The Christian must . . . requite . . . hostility with love. His behavior must be determined not by the way others treat him, but by the treatment he himself receives from Jesus."

—Dietrich Bonhoeffer

As expected, not everyone wanted to pray or talk about religion with a chaplain. I understood. Individuals can be sensitive about discussing personal beliefs. Even though people turned me down at times, I continued to offer prayer and warmth, privately or publicly. Over time, they warmed up to my visits, my mini-sermons, and my prayers, and returned warmth and affection—even the tough guys. Everyone needed consolation in some way, and it was my mission to be there for them, if only to listen to their gripes.

I made it a point to befriend everyone. Because I'm a hugger, I got teased, sometimes mercilessly. I cared about folks and showed it. However, not everyone wanted to hug at Ground Zero. I tried to be alert for non-huggers and never let that be a deterrent for caring for them or talking with them. Non-huggers received the hearty handshake. Hugging and handshaking became the norm for my visits.

When I talked to someone for the first time, I tried to learn their name. This, of course, involved discipline, and even with concentrated attention, I still got it wrong. Even so, when I remembered a name or two, the outcomes of a conversation amazed me.

"It's easy to remember my name," I told them. "My parents knew at birth I was dyslexic, so they named me Bob. I can always spell my name correctly, backward or forward."

When I first approached people around the perimeter or on the Pile, I occasionally sensed the guards or recovery workers thinking, "Let's get this over with and get on with things to be done."

Sometimes I overheard comments like, "Oh, here comes 'The Hugger'," or "Watch out! He hugs." Or worse yet: "Oh, no. Here comes Chaplain Bob." Whether it was my name or another chaplain's name, no matter. We all hated hearing, "Oh, no, it's *that* chaplain."

No matter what happens in life, I'll pray for others. I'll continue to hug people and pray for them as long as they allow me to do so. At the Pile, it was easy to be friendly. Many were receptive to prayer, some weren't. I understood this and respected their feelings. I prayed silently for those who struggled and were unable yet to express their pain.

We chaplains wanted to be there for them when they needed us. I wanted to provide a good shoulder to lean or cry on for anybody who needed relief or comfort. Some needed support, others didn't.

We all have our strengths, and we definitely have our weaknesses. When I felt weak, helpless, downtrodden, beaten up, or discouraged, I turned to my God in prayer Who gave me strength and courage to serve others.

SECTION 6

Comfort the Brokenhearted

"I think 9/11 was intended as evil, but I think through the mercy of God and through the courage of human beings and communities and leaders, we can make something out of it. It's always the way life is. It unfolds and things happen, but how we respond is really what's important."

—Reverend Lyndon Harris

25

Mourners at Ground Zero

"Grief is not an enemy or a sign of weakness. It is a sign of being human. Grief is the cost of loving someone."

—Bill Dunn and Kathy Leonard

Grieving families, friends, and associates felt compelled to visit Ground Zero. None visited out of morbid curiosity, but to be close to the place where their loved ones died. They vented, cried, hugged, and expressed deep pain and profound sorrow at the site. Envisioning their child or spouse or friend buried in this massive burial field shattered their hearts, and even the strongest shed tears.

We chaplains tried to bring a measure of comfort to these crushed people by escorting them to a designated site for dedications and mini-memorials for their loved ones. These ceremonies went on for hours. So many heartbroken people wanted to say goodbye. With room for only so many to crowd onto the designated platform, chaplains went back and forth to the perimeter to greet each new family or group and escort them out to the viewing spot.

The chaplain's job at this point was simple: Be there. Be sincere. Listen. Be ready to pray. Offer to read Scripture. Offer comfort. When appropriate, based on the families' expressed needs, bear witness to God's eternal love for everyone. Mourners remember those vulnerable moments and how tenderness affected them. They won't remember the words said, however, they will recall the feeling of compassion.

These grieving folks shared unbearable pain and sorrow, as well as the desire to talk about their hopes for their loved ones' bright futures, now vaporized. Talking about their loved ones brought fragments of solace even as pain stirred in their hearts. As I listened, they talked of shattered dreams and plans. Still numbed by shock, these families demonstrated such courage and strength.

As we walked to the overlook spot, some family members talked about their loved one: "What a wonderful sister she was," or "What a great mom she was." Dads spoke with pride: "My son was a football player," or "My son was good in academics." "He loved to sing." Friends spoke, "She loved her children so much." "She was such a good friend."

Families shared stories of musical talents, hobbies, honors, and accomplishments of those they desperately missed. America lost so many talented people on 9/11.

Not every mourner was quiet in their grief. Many raised their fists and voices, yelling obscenities into the dark chasms and black pits, cursing the terrorists, wailing out the pain in their hearts. More than a few needed this loud verbal release. Some ranted articulately without embarrassment, with no thought of political or social correctness. They spoke angry, hurtful words that others, in their quiet dignity and overwhelming misery, could not express.

As we led these memorials beside the vast debris field of death, families gained a better sense of the tragedy's magnitude. They imagined the terror their loved ones experienced in their last few moments, hoping they did not suffer. As they grieved or reflected in prayer, individuals connected with loved ones at this viewing spot.

Mourners carried beautiful flowers to throw onto the debris. Some threw flowers as a bunch. Every bouquet tossed into that wasteland— an expression of their love. Others tossed flower petals, one by one, as if to extend their time of closeness with their loved one at their gravesite. Their pain—too real, too raw, too new—gripped my heart with overflowing compassion. As we served these mourners, chaplains experienced the dichotomy of feeling hope and compassion for each family alongside horror and disbelief.

At times, I spoke during memorials; other times, I remained silent. Mourners often overlooked my presence. The horror of the untimely loss consumed their attention. So close to the place of the violent demise of their loved ones, they realized the significance and global impact of this event. With arms linked and heads bowed, tears flowed. Confronted by overwhelming loss, these people grasped onto each other.

When invited to do so, I shared Scripture. People appreciated this verse from Psalm 116:15 (NLT): *"The LORD's loved ones are precious to Him; it grieves Him when they die."* God counts each person as precious. Many tried to memorize this verse as they stood overlooking the ruins of the World Trade Center. Many families asked for me to read the most requested Scripture passage at Ground Zero, Psalm 23: *"The LORD is my shepherd."* The powerful words of this psalm contributed to a measure of peace.

When the family requested prayer, I implored God: "You're such an awesome God. Thank You for the privilege of sharing in prayer with this devastated family. I ask for Your tender touch on these folks as they mourn and say their goodbyes. They have so many wonderful memories of their loved ones, and I know they treasure them. Please give them peace and tender hugs to hold them through this time in their lives. Guide them and use them to help others who may need a hug or just a caring word to help them in their sorrow. Place a protective angelic hedge around them and keep them in Your care. Thank You for this time together. In Your precious name. Amen."

I saw kind, gentle people in those memorial moments. Their voices flowed with love and prayers for others. As raw and painful as it was to see these families grieve, their bone-deep sorrow gave me a deeper understanding of the fragility and value of life. I choked back my tears as I reflected on Psalm 34:17-19: *"The righteous cry, and the Lord hears and delivers them out of all their troubles. The Lord is near to the brokenhearted and saves those who are crushed in spirit. Many are the afflictions of the righteous, but the Lord delivers him out of them all."*

2 6

Silent Man's Torment

"Tears are words the heart can't express."

—Author Unknown

One morning, after my morning Bible reading and prayer, I went out to the breakfast buffet line at St. Paul's Chapel. A young firefighter with slumped shoulders and a forlorn look caught my attention.

As I moved with the line to obtain my meal, I watched him choose his food. He didn't say a word, just pointed at the food on the steam table: scrambled eggs, sausage, potatoes. Volunteers placed the servings on his plate.

To keep an eye on him, I followed him and sat nearby in a seat along the side of the hall a few tables away. He sat motionless, head bent over his plate, not eating a morsel of food. As I watched, I prayed to God to open an opportunity for me to share or talk with him. He sat in silence for well over an hour, not moving an inch, as his breakfast grew cold in front of him.

After about an hour of him sitting in this catatonic state, I moved over and sat closer to him. Another hour passed. Finally, I said, "I'm Chaplain Bob. Can I pray about something for you?"

He remained silent, staring at his plate. We sat side by side for another two hours with no words spoken. I experienced what Psalms 39:2-3 describes: *"But when I was silent and still, not even saying anything good, my anguish increased. My heart grew hot within me, and as I meditated, the fire burned."*

Stymied by his silence, I prayed silently. *God, please help me here. I feel helpless. This young man is hurting. How can I help him? What can I say to reach through his despondency and touch his heart? How can I bring a spark of hope to him in his misery?*

I spoke again. "I'm a Chicago firefighter. I'll stay here as long as you need me."

He turned, looked at me and choked out three words:

"They're.

All.

Dead."

Then he wept from such a deep place that his lament frightened me. Sobs wracked his body. His agony appeared to lie far beyond any help I could possibly offer. At a loss for words, I continued to pray silently.

After a few more minutes, I prayed aloud. "Dear God, please give this young man strength in this time of unbearable suffering and sorrow."

I leaned over, slid my arm around his shoulder and gave him a strong side hug. He turned and hugged me back. Between sobs, he thanked me for staying with him and praying for him. We talked until he announced, "I need to return to work." I never saw this fellow again.

This encounter provided a profound lesson, and I was grateful the Lord provided wisdom and insight. As difficult as it was to feel so helpless, I stayed beside him because it was not about my feelings, but about his struggle with the battle in his heart. Being a Chicago firefighter may have given me some street credibility with him as he opened up a little after I revealed that to him.

I'd also faced fires and flames and smoke, and yes, I'd suffered the anguish of the death of a fellow firefighter. And, yes. That was horrible. Good-hearted, well-meaning people often find it difficult to offer the gift of quiet presence and time to an individual in deep mourning. While uncomfortable, offering time and support can be the most amazing gift we give to help someone move one small step forward on their private journey of mourning.

2 7

Cell Phone Girl's Guilt

"Give sorrow words; the grief that does not speak knits up the o-er wrought heart and bids it break."

—William Shakespeare, *Macbeth*

No end of people laid bare their 9/11 stories to clear their hearts and minds, if only for a brief time. One evening I returned bone weary to St. Paul's Chapel. I melted into a pew, feeling totally useless, too tired to climb the stairs and find my little cot on the second floor to get some proper sleep. I closed my eyes and lay my head on the back of the pew; my feet sprawled out in front of me.

As I rested, a pretty, young woman in her late twenties, a volunteer at St. Paul's, approached me and asked, "Can we talk?"

She was like a little kid, timidly coming to me to ask for a bedtime story. Recognizing her as someone scarred by a terrible experience, I invited her to sit down.

"I missed her call," she said in a soft, shaky voice. "My best friend called me, and I missed her call. She worked in the World Trade Center, and she tried to reach me on my cell phone. I can't believe I didn't get her call. I rarely missed her calls. We talked every day on the phone, sometimes several times a day. Why didn't I pick up the phone? What was I doing that I didn't hear my phone ring?"

She stopped talking to regain her composure. "Then when I realized she called and what was going on at the Twin Towers I tried to call her back but couldn't get through. I called and called. She was on the 90th floor of Tower 1, the first one hit by the terrorists. I missed her last call. I let her down. She needed to talk to me in the last moments of her life, and I missed her call. How can I ever forgive myself?"

She fell against me and cried her heart out. I wrapped my arm around her shoulders and held her hand. I felt the warmth of her tears as they ran down her face. This poor, sweet woman couldn't bear the fact that she didn't have one last conversation with her friend. She suffered from the false guilt of abandoning her friend in her greatest moment of terror by not answering her phone.

It was pointless to explain that communication systems broke down in the attack, that pipes burst in the equipment room of the Verizon Building disrupting service to millions in New York City, or that others experienced the same difficulty connecting with their loved ones in the doomed towers. Offering a rational fact served no purpose. Explanations of the obvious never help. In her heart, she already perceived these facts. Facts, like empty words and platitudes, cannot help the grieving heart. Only compassionate presence makes a difference.

Sitting on the hard pews in the chapel, she talked through her pain and sadness, even so, this young woman faced some tough days ahead. I offered her some prayer. After talking a bit longer, she thanked me for listening and left.

As she departed, I noticed a line of folks gathered near my pew waiting to speak to me. Instead of resting, I met with many others. I don't remember all the stories, but I remember listening to broken people with heavy hearts, fractured spirits, and raw emotions who just needed to talk.

That was and is the hard part of being a chaplain in a crisis. So many people need to talk, so many will contend with long-term issues, and time does not work in our favor. I spent a few minutes or a few hours with each person, knowing we'd never meet again, but still prayed they'd find comfort.

28

Mother Is Waiting

"Panic and terror aren't the only kinds of fear. There are deeper kinds, more terrible kinds. Apprehension and heavy, heavy dread."

—Veronica Roth, *The Traitor*

How many mothers waited in vain for their sons or daughters to come home on September 11th? How many fathers received a phone call from their first responder child before racing into the inferno? How many heard their last "I love you" from the other end of the phone? How many spouses set dinner on the table, waiting for their husband or wife to walk through the door? How many days did they wait in limbo and agony to receive the news their loved one was never coming home again? How many waited to receive partial remains or no remains at all? How many never recovered emotionally enough to function in their new normal?

Standing and talking with a group of firefighters on my first tour of duty at Ground Zero, I noticed a tall gentleman in dusty pants and sweatshirt exhibiting unusual behavior. He walked a few steps and stopped to inspect the Pile, and then peered intently at the rubble around him. He stared at the faces of anyone who walked near him because in their gear they all looked alike from the side and back. Occasionally, he grabbed a shoulder or a sleeve of a firefighter or police office and turned them to look into their faces. Each time he shook his head back and forth and then started his unsteady walk again.

His eyes scoured the Pile, looking at the teams of workers who from this distance looked like ants on the gargantuan 16-acre, stories-high hellscape as they manipulated and dragged debris. Relentless noise assaulted our ears: shouting voices; beep, beep, beeping heavy equipment backing up; crashing thuds as heavy steel beams dropped from the jaws of cranes into the beds of waiting flatbed trucks; crackling and hissing fire and steam. The Pile vibrated with all this clamor and movement, but nothing—not the cacophony or the quaking pile—disturbed this gentleman's stumbling search.

Something is wrong. I walked over to him. "Can I help you?"

He grabbed my arm and gestured at the destruction. "Can you help me find my sons? One is a firefighter, and the other is a police officer. Mother is waiting for them at home."

I brought him over to the recovery workers. One of them informed me, "He's a retired firefighter." His pain pierced their hearts. However, they couldn't help him find his sons. They allowed me to take him further into Ground Zero.

We walked around the Pile for at least an hour, stopping each firefighter and police officer we met. He recognized none. Finally he stopped, drooped against me, and wrapped his arms around me.

His body convulsed. "They're dead, aren't they? My sons."

How do you respond to a grieving father in pain beyond anything I'd ever witnessed? Even as a chaplain who loved to talk, I struggled to respond. There were no right words.

"Yes," I said, "They probably are."

After that, we spent more time talking. I listened as he told me stories about his sons, how they were good boys who gave and received much love. "They made Mother and me so proud. They were our badge of honor. They loved their jobs. They loved fighting fires and helping people. They saved many lives in their work. I was sure I'd find the two of them alive and well and helping in the recovery effort."

Later I heard this father redirected his pain into purpose, providing compassionate care for the workers on the Pile. When someone looked discouraged, he offered comfort. He desired to help others cope with their pain, and he mourned with those who mourned.

Our heavenly Father experienced this same kind of anguish. He lost His only Son through an agonizing death on the cross. Because God experienced our pain, He offers comfort to us in our sorrow. Second Corinthians 1:3-5 spells it out for us: *"Blessed be the God and Father of our Lord Jesus Christ, the Father of mercies and God of all comfort, Who comforts us in all our affliction so that we will be able to comfort those who are in any affliction with the comfort with which we ourselves are comforted by God. For just as the sufferings of Christ are ours in abundance, so also our comfort is abundant through Christ."*

29

Fear of Flying

"No one ever told me that grief felt so like fear."

—C. S. Lewis

Ministry sometimes occurs in unexpected moments and at inconvenient times. The Bible advises us *"to always be ready to give an answer for the hope that is within us."* (1 Peter 3:15) This hope and belief empowered me to endure in difficult times.

After one tour at Ground Zero, overwhelmed and drained of every ounce of energy, I flew back to Chicago. I raced through the airport in my firefighters' turnout gear, my World Trade Center credentials around my neck, hoping to catch my flight, and thankful my outfit and credentials helped speed the process to reach the departure gate.

I anticipated catching a brief snooze on the two-hour trip—a nap to regain a little energy before reuniting with my wife and girls. I laid my head back against the headrest, closed my eyes, felt the vibration of the plane on takeoff, and promptly nodded off asleep.

Within minutes, a flight attendant woke me. "I'm sorry to bother you, but we lost friends in the planes hijacked on 9/11. Could you come to the back of the plane for a moment and talk with the flight attendants?"

Usually when people say they want to 'speak for a moment,' I know our talk will turn into an hour or more. Exhausted and half-asleep, I whispered a brief prayer for wisdom, strength, and patience. As a chaplain, I don't have all the answers. Suffering people do not want or need problem-solving or pat answers to their emotional stressors. They just want someone to listen to their anguish.

I walked to the back of the plane and met with the flight attendants. The men and women gathered there hugged me while struggling to hold back their tears. Each thanked me for my time at Ground Zero.

The attendants expressed their anxiety about flying. Their memories of lost friends—what their friends' last moments must have been like—haunted each person. They wanted to talk with someone close to the tragedy who understood the depth of their fears and sorrows. Several flight attendants worried about potential threats and more plane hijackings by terrorists. A few considered leaving their jobs. Feeling anxious, they scrutinized the faces and actions of passengers on each flight who might want to use their plane as a missile or weapon. As the flight attendants aired their fears and sorrows, they relaxed a little.

The flight time elapsed quickly with shared memories of their friends in better times, a few prayers, and many hugs and tears. The flight attendants took a little collection of money for me to take back to St. Paul's Chapel. I gave the crew members Ground Zero crosses, wished them well, and assured them, "I'll keep you in my prayers."

Their stories lodged in my memory, reminding me once again that we interact with many people in our lives. However, when we open up to each other, we connect on a heart level. Many people we encounter store within themselves unexpressed heartaches. One moment of vulnerability with a caring person softens the jagged edge of pain, at least for a few moments.

As I exited the plane, many passengers patted me on the back or offered to buy me coffee. Some requested prayer. Others offered prayer. This type of 9/11 bonding happened on several of my flights to and from Chicago and New York City.

On another flight and after our plane landed, a pilot asked me to talk with him in the rear of the plane. He shared his worries about potential terrorist dangers, passenger fears, and airline employees' anxieties. What changes for safety and security would FAA authorities make? This pilot wasn't personally acquainted with anyone on the crashed planes, but considered all those lost to be part of his airline family.

Airline pilots and flight attendants struggled with the same questions everyone else asked and faced the same fears. They also wanted to hear details about my work on the Pile. I tried to keep the stomach-churning details out of the stories, but sometimes they asked for more of the gruesome details. Sometimes they regretted that choice. Even so, we connected with one another, and in some small way helped ease the profound ache in each other's hearts.

SECTION 7

Hope in the Midst of Tragedy

"That the [Teddy] bears were appreciated by adults soon became apparent to Lucarelli [who collected bears for traumatized school children] once she began volunteering at St. Paul's. 'Big, huge, tree-like guys wanted them. They snapped them up faster than the kids,' said Lucarelli. 'They put them in their helmets and pockets.'"

—Jane Flanagan

30

Big Daddy Answers Prayer

"If you're an underdog, mentally disabled, physically disabled, if you don't fit in, if you're not as pretty as the others, you can still be a hero."

—Steve Guttenberg

On one of my tours at Ground Zero late in the fall, I was close to depleting my stash of wooden Ground Zero crosses. I hadn't been able to connect with the woman from New Jersey who made the original crosses, so I debated about what to do. One day, during my morning quiet time with my Bible and prayer before breakfast at St. Paul's, I pleaded with God for more crosses: *"Okay, Big Daddy, here I am again begging for something. . . again. I need more crosses today. I have almost none left to give out, and these crosses touch people's hearts and remind them of Your love for them. So, God, the ball is in Your court. Thanks for Your help. You are an amazing God, and I know You will answer this prayer. Amen."*

Maybe the prayer was a bit irreverent, but my God's shoulders were big enough to handle my request. I kept this appeal solely between God and me. I rose up from the pew, walked ten feet out the side door of the sanctuary to the breakfast buffet and joined those already in line. Within seconds, I felt a gentle tap on my shoulder. I turned to find a man and woman behind me.

"Are you Chaplain Bob?" the man asked.

"Yes." *Who is this man, and how does he know me?* "Can I help you?"

He introduced himself as a pastor from Barstow, California. He and his wife handed me several large boot boxes. "A member of our church met you here on the perimeter. You prayed with him and gave him a Ground Zero cross. He thought you might need more. Take a look in these boxes."

I opened the first box. Inside I found a motley collection of handmade Popsicle stick crosses. Not the fanciest crosses by a long shot, and not as fine as those made by the woman in New Jersey. Even so, I was amazed.

The pastor gestured to the boxes. "Children and adults with special needs made these crosses. They wanted everyone in New York City to know California is praying for them, and God loves them. Can you use these?"

As I hugged him, salty gratitude deluged my eyes. "Just moments ago, I begged God to send more crosses, and He answered that prayer."

This sobering, clear answer to my prayer shook me. Ashamed I flippantly told God, "The ball is in Your court." I bowed my head and offered a prayer of thanks. But really, God answered my prayer weeks before I even asked for more crosses.

Those special, precious people in California—the "least of these" who occupy the least influential, least spectacular rungs on the social ladder—glued together Popsicle stick crosses, painted them with bright colors, and sprinkled them with glitter. Some crosses, glued awkwardly together, looked like X's instead of T's. Some sported globs of glue and paint. But each one was a keepsake made by a childlike heart full of love.

As I passed these crosses out to the heroes at Ground Zero, I related how I acquired them, and who made them. Some recipients wept and hugged me. They poured out gratitude for what the crosses represented and for the thoughtful special children and adults who produced them. Even now the memory stirs powerful emotions in my heart.

This clear example of God answering my prayers almost frightened me. *God is so near.*

Then I thought, again, maybe a bit too flippantly, *That was easy. How about a shiny new BMW? No, I'd better not ask for that. That's too brazen, too sacrilegious.*

Changing my attitude, I added, *"Thank You, Lord, for giving me what I need and not what I want."*

The Bible affirms many promises regarding prayer. When I thought about these caring children, these verses in *Philippians 4:6-7* flashed through my mind: *"Be anxious for nothing, but in everything by prayer and supplication with thanksgiving let your requests be made known to God. And the peace of God, which surpasses all comprehension, will guard your hearts and your minds in Christ Jesus."*

31

Candle Man: Sad Man, Big Heart

"How far that little candle throws its beams! So shines a good deed in a naughty world."

—William Shakespeare

"Chaplain Bob, we need candles," Sister Grace said to me one day at St. Paul's Chapel. "We've almost run out of them, and we need them to keep soft lighting in the sanctuary where workers and volunteers rest. We need them ASAP. What can you do?"

I searched all around the neighboring city blocks to find one open shop that might sell candles. Countless shops and businesses around Ground Zero closed because of the 9/11 attacks. Unable to carry out their normal business activities and earn their income, shop owners suffered.

As I walked, I prayed. *Lord, I need candles. Lots of them. These candles provide comfort to the weary search and recovery workers and volunteers who come to rest at St. Paul's. Help me find an open shop with candles for sale. Thank You in advance for answering my prayers.*

Several blocks away, I found a single shop with its door wide open. The owner had tried to clean the thick layers of ash, dirt, and grime from the glass-topped counters and tiled floors. The clean-up appeared unfinished. He sat near the doorway, hunched over, head in hands, elbows on knees, unable to swipe off one more surface.

I'd seen many sad people in my tours at Ground Zero, but this man radiated an impression that he carried an extra-heavy burden of despair. His world, like everyone else's, was in turmoil; his source of income wiped out.

After greeting him, I asked, "How are you holding up?"

At first, he didn't answer or look up. I sat down on a bench near him, and he finally said, "I'm not open for business."

"That's okay," I said. "You look like you need a friend. May I sit with you for a bit?"

"Okay."

We then talked for a long time about the attacks and the devastation and his feelings and how it affected his family. After a while, his mood lightened a bit, and I changed the subject. "I'm on a mission. I've looked everywhere for candles for St. Paul's Chapel, but I can't find any."

His face lit up, and he stood and motioned to me. "Follow me, my friend."

We walked to the back room. "You want candles?" He pointed to his storage shelving. "I've got candles."

Hundreds of candles in bags and boxes lined the shelves—from tea lights to candlesticks to Yankee candles, scented candles and unscented candles, box upon box.

He smiled. "Help yourself. Take all you can carry."

"What can I pay you?"

He waved his hand. "No, no. Just come back when you need more."

"Can we pray together?" I asked. He agreed. We bowed our heads, prayed, then wished each other well. I hugged him, loaded myself up with candles and left.

Ironic. Not one single shop was open for business in these ash-covered streets around Ground Zero, nor were any other business owners around. I entered this one particular shop with its door open and started talking with this solitary man, and he supplied enough candles to keep St. Paul's Chapel in soothing light for a good, long time.

God answered my prayer in a big way. I carried the candles back to Sister Grace and told her about the Candle Man. Sister Grace smiled, not surprised in the least by either happening: finding a man who needed compassionate care, or getting the candles—free, no less.

After that, people started calling me Bob the Scrounger. I chuckled at that nickname.

As always, Sister Grace's candle-finding mission reminded me that spending time connecting with a suffering person on a personal level may light a flicker of hope in their dark hopelessness. Asking for a small favor or action can turn despair into care, extinguishing their overwhelming sadness and igniting a sense of purpose and value.

32

A Little Child's Gift

"It's not how much we give but how much love we put into giving."

—Mother Teresa

One evening while walking the perimeter and talking with those gathered along the fences, I passed a young family of four visiting New York City. I overheard the dad say to his young daughter and son, "Here comes a hero."

I turned and looked to see where he pointed. Nodding his head up and down, he pointed to me, and said, "You're a hero to all of us. Everyone who works here is a hero to the rest of us. I want my children to get a close-up look at the brave workers inside the perimeter. I can't imagine the hell those workers are going through. I've seen pictures, but I'm having trouble wrapping my head around it."

Even though he failed to grasp the vastness of the situation himself, this father wanted his children to see first-hand this important chapter in our country's history. His little blond-haired daughter, maybe six years old, all bundled up against the cold in her red, woolly coat hugged her well-worn Teddy bear. She turned to me and asked, "What do you do here?"

"I pray for the people who work here cleaning up this big mess. I take water or food to them when they're thirsty or hungry. I listen to their stories about their families or the work they're doing. Sometimes they're too tired to talk, so I let them rest their head on my shoulder, or I just give them a pat on the shoulder or a hug."

"Oh," she said, "That's what my daddy does for me when I'm tired."

Out of the mouths of babes fall gems of truth. Like the hand of God offering comfort, she grasped the goal of my ministry.

Tears filled my eyes. Adults often overlook the simple, obvious things in life, like offering a shoulder to cry on for someone who's heartbroken and weary.

After a minute, the little girl held her precious Teddy bear up. "Here," she said. "Give this to a soldier. Tell him it's for his little girl." Her eyes teared up as she handed over her stuffed bear to pass on to another child.

"That Teddy bear is her favorite toy," her mom said. "She takes it everywhere she goes."

That moment in time burned into my memory. Ground Zero taught all sorts of lessons to all of us, young and old, workers and visitors. Sometimes those lessons emerged from the wisest of all: little children with tender hearts. This little girl gave up her most precious possession in the world. She was the brave one.

We gathered in a family hug and said a prayer together, "Thank You, Lord, for precious little children who know when another little child needs a special gift and some caring. And thank You for welcoming little children into Your presence and promising that 'the kingdom of heaven belongs to such as these.' Amen."

I shared this story with a young female guard, and she accepted the Teddy bear to take home to her daughter. She promised to tell her child the story of the generous little girl who gave away her most prized possession.

In Luke 21, a widow placed her mite—two small copper coins worth about one-fifth of a penny—in the collection plate at the temple treasury in Jerusalem. Jesus noticed her sacrifice and said, *"Truly I say to you, this poor widow put in more than all of them; for they all out of their surplus put into the offering; but she out of her poverty put in all that she had to live on."* (Luke 21:3-4)

This extravagant gift given from the generous heart of a compassionate child touched the heart of a mother working long hours in the dreadful conditions of the Pile. The little girl's sacrifice of her Teddy bear comforted her lonely child.

Never underestimate what you can do to help a suffering person. Small gestures can be the noblest, kindest, and most caring actions that reap big results.

SECTION 8

Rescue for the Rescuers

"Here [in New York City after 9/11] it feels as if everyone is working together for the common good. It is an experience of love and community unlike any I have ever seen. And to me it signals the presence of the Holy Spirit. For it is the Holy Spirit that brings unity and concord, that causes peace and harmony, that banishes division and strife."

—Father James Martin, *Searching for God at Ground Zero*

33

Angels of Mercy
Answer the Call

"Alone we can do so little, together we can do so much."

—Helen Keller

Skilled volunteers from all walks of life and all occupations served our Ground Zero heroes at St. Paul's: physical therapists, massage therapists, podiatrists, nurses, counselors, musicians, chefs, teachers and lawyers, even stockbrokers and federal judges. Unless we asked, we never knew what some of them did in their professional lives. They pitched in with their hearts and souls and talents to accomplish what needed to be done, no matter how mundane or difficult.

These dedicated service providers used vacation time, financed their travel, and sacrificed time away from families and normal, everyday life to serve in New York City. Everyone wanted to help in any way they could. Important work awaited them at St. Paul's: answering phones, taking messages, sweeping, mopping, cleaning toilets, folding blankets and placing them in the pews, cooking, serving food, and greeting and encouraging other volunteers and workers. They plastered letters, cards, drawings, posters, and giant banners of prayers and encouraging messages all over the walls and balconies of St. Paul's Chapel, an art gallery of prayers from people around the world. They distributed prayer letters and stuffed animals on cots where exhausted workers slept. These kind-hearted efforts elicited smiles and more than a few tears from tough, burly recovery workers.

Donations streamed in every day. Like stock people in a supermarket, volunteers shelved toothpaste, toothbrushes, mouthwash, deodorant, hygiene products, ChapStick, soap, aspirin, ointments, Band-Aids, medical supplies, socks, work gloves, and hundreds of other items needed by workers and volunteers. Cases of soda pop and water towered on the sidewalk outside St. Paul's.

A truckload of work boots arrived from an emergency-supplies company. Cartons of heavy work socks arrived from another source. A 16-wheeler big rig filled with Teddy bears arrived from Arizona. Quick-thinking people sent dog food for search and rescue dogs. Firefighting equipment and monetary donations flowed into neighborhood fire stations and to other emergency services providers around Ground Zero. From all over America, people helped in any way possible.

Once in a while, a new crew of bright-eyed, bushy-tailed volunteers turned up at the chapel. Katherine Avery, a St. Paul's staff member, welcomed these volunteers and advised them about procedures. She occasionally asked me or other chaplains to share insights about the work and how volunteers could help.

By choice, some volunteers never went to the perimeter or the Pile. Others gathered the courage to venture over. But all of them asked questions.

"If you do go over to the Pile, you'll see a lot of emotional pain," I warned. "You'll see people on the verge of sheer exhaustion. You'll see spontaneous hugs and laughter and lots of tears. Just be ready to listen to anyone who needs to talk. Let them talk and don't interrupt. Telling how the attacks affected them personally gives their sorrow words. After their avalanche of pain tumbles out, express your gratitude for their willingness to do the gruesome recovery work."

I cautioned them, "You might experience emotional highs and lows. Sitting with a suffering soul and hearing their agonizing stories of finding a friend's mutilated human remains will be distressing." To process pain and begin the journey to regain emotional margin, many sufferers needed to tell and retell their stories. Volunteers provided supportive listening ears.

"As much as possible," I advised them, "maintain a cheerful attitude without being phony. Help workers find food, clothing, bedding, and other essentials. But if and when you feel overwhelmed, acknowledge those feelings and talk to someone. No person escapes the emotional roller coaster associated with this tragedy."

God sent these volunteers, angels of mercy, to minister to our Ground Zero heroes. We all appreciated the time and love they expressed and the caring their actions demonstrated. Under the worst of circumstances, kind and compassionate people gave their all.

Thank you to all who gave a part of yourselves at St. Paul's Chapel and at other service areas around Ground Zero. I will never forget you. I salute your Christian love and attitudes. God bless all of you. And to the people who were unable to help onsite, we appreciated your well wishes and prayers, your notes and cards, and your donated items. You'll never know how much you meant to all of us.

34

Relieving Aches and Pains

"We must find the time to stop and thank the people who make a dif-ference in our lives."

—John F. Kennedy

One night during a wintry tour of duty, I suffered from a miser-able head cold. After an hour of sniffling and coughing, I rolled out of my cot and launched a search-and-find mission to obtain some Nyquil. I scanned the chapel tables carpeted with donated aspirin, anal-gesics, toothpaste, and other over-the-counter medications. No Nyquil. I checked with Sister Grace and other volunteers, but they said, "Sorry, no Nyquil." I resigned myself to a fitful sleep.

"Hold on a minute," Sister Grace told me. She grabbed a nearby vol-unteer. "Run to the drugstore and get some Nyquil for Chaplain Bob."

The volunteer scurried off and soon returned with the medicine.

Touched by this kindness, I thanked the volunteer and downed the Nyquil capsules, and then crawled back under the warm, woolly blanket on my cot. After a few minutes, I fell asleep, thankful for the ministering angels at St. Paul's who blessed me with their care.

Aches and pains didn't last long at St. Paul's. An incredible team of massage therapists, chiropractors, podiatrists, and other medical personnel, stood ready 24/7 to soothe physical traumas. I marveled at the care and deep concern these volunteer professionals invested in their work.

One day, some building material under the surface of a debris pile gave way as I walked on it. I tripped and twisted my ankle, then hobbled back to St. Paul's for medical help. A podiatrist attended to me right away. He taped up my ankle, enabling me to continue my daily walks on the perimeter.

The massage therapists—volunteers from all over the country—worked almost around the clock. Ground Zero heros working on the Pile deserved to come first for massages, so I always waited until late at night to take my turn for getting relief for my aching muscles. If one of us fell asleep on the massage table, the therapists let us sleep, perhaps guessing that if we woke up, we'd go right back to the Pile where people needed us.

No matter how tired these professionals grew, they never complained or sent anyone away. How unusual to receive bill-free, top-tier medical care at a moment's notice. The memory of their care still touches my heart.

Because of the treacherous working conditions, stinging eyes, twisted ankles, blisters, bruises, scrapes, cuts, and burns became common complaints. In normal situations, we'd wait an hour in a doctor's office or emergency room. Volunteer nurses, health practitioners, and doctors converged from miles away, on call and available to serve us without any delay. Where can you receive that kind of immediate service?

Another time while ministering on the Pile, I sat on an exposed steel beam and pulled off my work boots to shake out accumulated grit and debris. In the process, I whacked my foot on a piece of exposed rebar. A blood blister formed under my big toenail and throbbed so painfully that I saw stars. I limped back to St. Paul's where yet another podiatrist treated me.

"I can stop the pain," she promised, "and the process won't hurt."

Skeptical, I relented. She released the pressure and blood under my big toe—and it didn't hurt one bit after that.

Not only were our physical aches and wounds cared for, but our emotional wounds also received restoration. Talented musicians and musical groups performed at St. Paul's. As they played the piano, harp, violin, or other instruments, the gift of their music soothed our traumatized spirits and relaxed our tense bodies.

God provided unlimited resources through individuals from all over the country who left the comfort of their homes to serve others. From the ashes of Ground Zero, a sense of community surged among these compassionate volunteers. Each one brought unique talents and used them to *"faithfully administer God's grace in its various forms."* (1 Peter 4:10)

35

Coffee, Lasagna, and Black Olives

"We pray for the big things and forget to give thanks for the ordinary, small (and yet really not small) gifts."

—Dietrich Bonhoeffer

"Would you like a cup of Dunkin' Donuts coffee?" a bystander outside the concrete barrier called out as I walked the perimeter early one cold morning.

Dunkin' Donuts coffee?

What heavenly words. A cup of steaming creamy coffee. What a luxury in this wasteland.

I approached the gentleman who offered the coffee and extended my hand to greet him. "Thank you. I love Dunkin' Donuts coffee. Lots of cream, no sugar, please."

When the coffee arrived, I sipped the hot brew slowly, savoring every drop—best cup of coffee I'd ever tasted. The smell reminded me of home. I didn't realize how much I took coffee for granted until I didn't have any.

This kind man told me the location of the Dunkin' Donuts shop not too far from St. Paul's, and I began frequenting their establishment.

126

They never accepted payment for my coffee, but I always left a fine tip for their kindness and generosity.

Time and schedules at Ground Zero held no meaning. Day merged into night. Night blended into day. The dawn-to-dark and back again clock of life ticked away into a borderless blur. Giant Hollywood stage lights glared from dusk to dawn. Normal mealtimes? Nonexistent. No regular bedtime. Nothing followed routine. The unusual and unexpected ruled our new normal.

Like many others at Ground Zero, I worked through mealtimes, often returning to St. Paul's from the Pile or perimeter at a late hour. On one such night, I sat in a pew gathering my thoughts and chatting with fellow, bone-weary workers. I'd missed another mealtime and wondered whether I could find something to eat. As if reading my mind, a young lady brought me a warm dinner of lasagna, mixed green salad with Italian dressing, homemade garlic bread juicy with butter and minced garlic, and black olives.

What a treat. How do they know I love lasagna? And black olives—my absolute, all-time favorite. I can devour a whole can of jumbo black olives at one sitting. This meal reminded me of home and eating a meal my loving wife prepared.

Such simple, kind gestures touched my heart and renewed my spirit. I felt loved by co-laborers at the chapel. The compassionate care of my fellow volunteers gave me courage and strength to keep up my ministry at Ground Zero.

36

Who Brushes a Dog's Teeth?

"A person without a sense of humor is like a wagon without springs . . .
jolted by every pebble on the road."

—Henry Ward Beecher

After walking the perimeter one day, I sat down in the pews at St. Paul's with a few firefighters to take a breather. We pulled family pictures from our wallets and passed them around. Each firefighter shared tender stories about their sons and daughters, moments of pride and hilarious mishaps. The camaraderie brightened our moods. Our children represented hope for the future.

One firefighter shared about the time he and his wife spent hours painting the walls of their living and dining rooms. Exhausted but satisfied after a hard day's work, they sat down for a cup of coffee in the kitchen. A few minutes later their five-year-old daughter, bubbly with excitement, pranced into the room. "Mommy, Daddy—Come look!"

They followed her into the living room—and discovered crayon drawings all over one newly painted wall. "Look at my pretty pictures."

We laughed and enjoyed the silly humor of it all. "It wasn't funny then," he said, "but we laugh about it now."

I told him of a time when my daughters were very young. Early one morning after an all-nighter at the fire station and still grimy and sweaty from a rough shift, I went into the bathroom to brush my teeth and clean up. My toothbrush was missing from its usual spot on the bathroom sink. Bewildered, I called to my wife. "Honey, have you seen my toothbrush?"

"Sorry," she told me. "Ask the girls."

I found Noelle, my oldest daughter, and asked, "Have you seen my toothbrush?"

"Oh, Dad, Heather used your toothbrush to brush the dog's teeth."

The dog?

Heather piped up. "Sorry, Dad—I brushed Fang's teeth with your toothbrush and forgot to put it back for you! I'll get it."

Ewwww. I just stared at her. Just how many times had Heather used my toothbrush on the dog and remembered to put it back? I was afraid to ask.

The firefighters and I belly laughed at the family stories. Others chimed in to tell about their humorous mishaps at home.

Like an injection of good medicine, laughter relieved tension and the heavy oppression and sadness we carried back to St. Paul's from the recovery work. Chaplains don't always preach and pray to touch other lives and hearts. Storytelling and camaraderie restores our hope, too.

Our work on the Pile and around the perimeter reminded me of the Israelites in Jerusalem in biblical times who were forced into captivity by the Babylonians. Marched off to a distant land, they wept bitterly mile after mile along their desert trek. (Psalm 126)

Years later when released from captivity, they ascended to Jerusalem singing, *"our mouths filled with laughter, our tongues with songs of joy."* They praised God for the great things He had done for them. Their deep sorrow changed into great happiness.

Likewise, our laughter in these desperate conditions softened our sorrows and infused a measure of hope back into our lives. While we weren't singing for joy in New York City, at least a humorous crack in the wall of oppression allowed hope to seep through.

37

New Underwear, Anyone?

"The things that truly define me can't be lost."

—Amy Neftzger, *The War of Words*

One morning, fresh from Chicago, I returned to Ground Zero for another tour of duty. When I walked into St. Paul's Chapel, a new bunch of volunteers greeted me. I parked my suitcase in my usual spot and told the volunteer in charge, "That suitcase is mine. I'll collect it after I do a prayer-walk on the perimeter."

"Okay," she said, "I'll keep an eye on it."

Hours later, hot and sweaty from working in my turnout gear, I returned to the chapel to shower and change into fresh clothes. My suitcase?

Gone.

Nowhere in sight.

I was crushed. Nobody knew where it was, and the volunteer who said she'd watch over my things left hours before.

Another sheepish volunteer confessed, "We opened that suitcase because we thought it was a donation, and we gave everything away to people who needed stuff."

The suitcase contained a new toothbrush (not the one Heather used to brush Fang's teeth), toothpaste, deodorant, brand new underwear, and a few changes of clothing. I'd also packed books from my Bible college classes with personal notes I'd used over my years in ministry.

After searching the donations area, we recovered my suitcase—but nothing else. The loss of my personal belongings changed my attitude a little. Although originally depressed over losing these basic material things, I managed fine without them.

The volunteers scrounged up toiletries for me, and I cleaned up. However, my beloved books never found their way back to me. From that experience, I vowed not let my possessions own me, and I hoped whoever found my books received a blessing from them.

The next day I looked around and wondered, *Hmmm, who's wearing my underwear now?*

38

Someone Is Sleeping in My Bed!

"Without oil the axle soon grows hot, and accidents occur; and if there be not a holy cheerfulness to oil our wheels, our spirits will be clogged with weariness."

—Charles Haddon Spurgeon

If not used and cared for properly, machines and equipment wear out. Constant use in adverse conditions results in mechanical failure and loss of productivity. Although an amazing and resilient machine, the human body also wears out physically, emotionally, and spiritually with overuse and improper care.

With no time clock on the Pile to tell workers when to start or finish work, time held no meaning at Ground Zero. At night, blazing lights flooded the debris field, enabling recovery and cleanup work to continue around the clock. This reminded me of Revelation 21:25: *"There is no night there."* This verse spoke of the New Jerusalem, or heaven, and emphasized the hope we have in our God, and the eternity He offers with Him. But this well-lit hellscape was definitely not heaven. More like a purgatory of affliction.

Everyone worked hours on end. We pushed our bodies to the limit—and then some. With no differentiation between day and night, our brains played tricks on us.

Like others, many times I was too bone-weary to fall asleep. One morning, I left the Pile around 2 a.m. and headed back to St. Paul's Chapel. A therapist gave me a relaxing massage, and I went to the upstairs cot I claimed as my own while in Manhattan.

Before leaving for the Pile that day, I'd left my personal stuff on my usual cot along with cards and notes kind volunteers left for me. But now, I approached my cot and saw a National Guardsman sprawled on it, sound asleep.

What's this? Someone sleeping in my bed? My annoyance quickly softened. *He's probably more exhausted than I am. I'll let him be.* I looked for an open cot, but didn't find one. Finally, I spread a blanket on the floor, poked earplugs in my ears, and fell asleep.

I slept for fifteen minutes or so before a chapel volunteer woke me.

"Someone requested a chaplain to come to the Pile," she said. "They found some more remains."

Searchers who recovered human body fragments needed comfort and prayer. Honored to minister, I dragged my aching, dead-tired body back to the Pile to conduct another mini-memorial service. Thankful for the power nap that renewed my strength, I spent a few more hours with folks who needed to express their sorrow and frustration.

SECTION 9

Caregiver Fatigue

"Internalized and unspoken—three years later—I still held on to un-healthy, immobilizing emotions: anger towards the perpetrators, guilt for surviving what others did not, trauma from the fear of imminent death when I was under attack, and a pervasive feeling that it was all so unfair . . . .self-loathing kicked in. It crippled me."

—Michael Benfante, *Reluctant Hero*

39

Sanctuary for Chaplains

"A brave man acknowledges the strength of others."

—Veronica Roth

In *Work of the Chaplain,* Naomi Paget and Janet McCormack offer this caution: "Intentionally choosing to walk alongside and share the burdens of people in need results in physical, emotional, and spiritual fatigue of the caregiver." When we chaplains needed sanctuary, we turned to fellow chaplains to share our personal anxieties and fears.

Chaplains from all over the U.S. showed up in the early months of cleanup work at Ground Zero, and we formed a close-knit group of ministers. We worked together, ate together, shared stories together, suffered together, and lifted each other up. A deep bond developed among us. We identified with each other and guided each other in ways which helped everyone to grow in ministry and personal spiritual journeys.

Each chaplain used their individual talents in wonderfully powerful ways at the site. I learned so much from these fine, seasoned chaplains, things I'd never learn from a book. I love academics and book learning, but there's nothing like raw on-the-job training and feet-to-the-fire experiences to prepare you for the unexpected in trauma situations. Gifted in their approaches, many of these men and women helped others move through pain on their journey toward recovery.

So many times, I sat with other ministers and listened intently as they shared stories of their pain and suffering. I needed shoulders to lean on, too. I found solace in conversations with other chaplains who served on the Pile. Group hugs, shared Scripture readings, hymn sings, and prayer brought comfort and some semblance of joy back to my shell-shocked heart.

Each day, we battled discouragement in this overwhelming mess. Seeing the recovery of mutilated human remains unsettled some chaplains. Others struggled with anger, tension, and frustration from not being able to do more for our fellow man. We lacked magical answers for all the questions we encountered about faith, religion, God, and suffering.

Many workers, volunteers, and chaplains agonized, struggling with indescribable pain. On one occasion, I observed from the sidelines, one visibly frustrated chaplain who tried to console a despondent man but failed. I recalled the times I'd tried to comfort someone beyond comfort and empathized with his look of helplessness.

Although I found it difficult not to step in, I held back. At last, the chaplain and the troubled man finished their conversation and parted ways. I approached the chaplain.

"How are you holding up?" I asked. Since we respected the confidentiality of every conversation, I didn't ask for any details of his counseling interaction.

His reply? An all too common look—despondency. Defeated and tired, the chaplain voiced words we all thought at one time or another. "What are we doing here? Are we helping anyone at all?"

The chaplain and I prayed together for peace and God-given strength for that broken man and also for ourselves. Another time, another place, another person might reach him, but at this point in his journey, he was unable to release his sorrow and anger.

Chaplains don't evaluate interchanges as successful or unsuccessful. We do the best we can in every counseling opportunity, while keeping in mind that we can't reach every person or solve every problem. We can only dig so deep to help others, and then we must surrender the person to the Lord. When comfort does not result from interacting with a hurting individual, we can't take it personally. We can make our requests for help known to God, and trust Him to follow up with additional help in His timing.

I cannot speak for other chaplains, but for me, Ground Zero was a very spiritual experience. As I served at the Pile, I tried to stay in deep reverent prayer and devotion each day. I wept with those who wept and laughed with those who laughed. I thought. *Wow, this is right out of Ecclesiastes. "There is an appointed time for everything. And there is a time for every event under heaven—A time to weep and a time to laugh; A time to mourn and a time to dance . . . A time for war and a time for peace . . . There is nothing better for [mankind] than to rejoice and to do good in one's lifetime . . . "* (Ecclesiastes 3:1, 4, 8, 12.)

I salute all the chaplains who lived and loved others at the Pile. God bless you, friends. I'd love to hunt you down, greet you, read Scripture with you, pray with you, sing with you, and love you even today. Always remember the Bible's promise, *"Then those who feared the Lord spoke to one another, and the Lord gave attention and heard it, and a book of remembrance was written before Him for those who fear the Lord and who esteem His name."* (Malachi 3:16)

40

Spilling and Mopping: Releasing Our Laments

"It is not the depth of our feelings that hurts us the most, but the strength of our resistance. Sometimes we have to let go."

—Author Unknown

At Ground Zero, no one escaped the emotional upheavals: firefighters, police officers, ironworkers, construction crews, clean-up crews, volunteers, . . . or chaplains.

Once in a while, chaplains bumped into each other on the Pile and spontaneously started a discussion about the workers, the true heroes of the Pile, and how they were holding up in their gruesome work. On rare occasions, these impromptu meetings led us to voice our pain and frustration. More often, though, we hid our feelings, trying to remain strong to support each other and all those around us.

But chaplains, too, needed time to release the emotions and anxieties we stifled while working in this calamitous turmoil. Scheduled private meetings for chaplains provided the opportunity to unburden ourselves with each other. But even though we understood the importance of sharing our emotional struggles, we still wrestled with whether to verbalize our pain. False bravado buried our internal torments and tangled nerves.

Some chaplains didn't attend these meetings, but others couldn't wait to vent. People familiar with me encouraged me—a master at holding my feelings tight within me—to show up.

Nobody wanted to be labeled "the crier" in the group or to be suspected of losing his grip on reality. Even so, within the safety net of our chaplain's group, many of us allowed our feelings to flow. Some spilled their pent-up emotions. Others mopped up. On many occasions, I spilled; other times, I mopped.

In a choking, trembling, and halting voice, one chaplain confessed how he spent hours on the Pile talking with the workers who struggled with some degree of depression or anxiety after finding remains. Curious himself, one time he looked at a recovered piece of human tissue but couldn't make out what it was.

He moved in closer for a better look. The sickly odor of death and the sight of a mangled piece of human flesh overwhelmed his senses and emotions, and he vomited. Even as he related his story, he gagged at the memory, lost his composure, and cried.

After that raw exposure to death, this chaplain berated himself for his morbid curiosity in the first place and harbored serious regrets about his ability to be on the Pile during further recoveries. We all grasped exactly what he talked about. We'd all experienced that same curiosity and regret. Soon after that meeting, he left Ground Zero. Each one of us understood the torment of his decision to leave.

As I walked away from one intense chaplains' meeting, another chaplain pressed his hand on my shoulder and asked, "Do you have a minute?"

"Sure," I said, and waited for his next thoughts.

"You're different," he said.

Uh, oh. Is that good or bad? I wondered what he meant by his comment.

He continued, "I can see the Spirit in you, brother." Then he leaned his head on my chest and burst into tears. With my arms around him, holding him, I, too, lost my composure.

Other chaplains noticed us and rushed to our aid, surrounding us in a group bear hug. The tenderness shown was so beautiful. Here we were, chaplains, grown men and one woman, in an arms-entangled bunch, loving each other, leaning on each other, sobbing together, and praying. No one tried to be strong.

We all admitted to emotional struggles and torment, but we helped each other handle the burden. Talking, crying, and praying released enough tension and discouragement to enable us to return to the Pile to carry this same comfort to others in need, just as 2 Corinthians 1:4 encourages us.

God heard our laments and listed our tears on His scroll. (Psalm 56:8) After that group release of pain, a few chaplains left the Pile when their tour commitments ended, and I never saw them again.

41

Wise Counsel,
Conflicting Opinions

"For you will certainly carry out God's purpose, however you act, but it makes a difference to you whether you serve like Judas or like John."

—C. S. Lewis

A t times, being at Ground Zero became a spiritual battleground. Not always of the same theological viewpoint, some chaplains' major or minor doctrinal differences caused occasional communication problems. Of course, we loved sharing our faith, but we only did this according to the rules set out by the authorities when we signed up as volunteer chaplains. Regardless of individual beliefs, we tried to minister to everyone with tenderness. When a person of a different faith wanted to speak with a clergy from their faith, we helped them connect with each other.

At Ground Zero, authorities told us, "Do not give religious advice of any kind unless an individual specifically asks for it." The authorities asked anyone who violated this directive to leave.

The majority of the chaplains followed this directive to the letter: We accepted and understood that our purpose on the Pile and on the perimeter was to offer comfort to those suffering. We showed God's love through our example and our words of compassion, just as Scripture points out: *"A new commandment I give to you, that you love one another, even as I have loved you, that you also love one another."* (John 13:34)

Peter Scholtes, a parish priest at St. Brendan's on the south side of Chicago, put the words of John 13:34 to music in his song entitled *They'll Know We Are Christians by Our Love.* People of faith sing the lyrics of his song as a gentle reminder of our responsibilities to love others as God loves us—unconditionally.

One minister showed up on the Pile one day and started lambasting volunteers and workers. "You're all going to hell unless you pray *right now* and repent of your sins." He aired his opinion about why all the people died in the Twin Towers collapse, and how the rest of us were going to die in this sinful pit. I failed to see the love of the Lord in his tone or diatribe. His continuous tirade stoked anger in workers and chaplains on the Pile. Thankfully, the authorities finally asked him to leave.

At Ground Zero, when workers, volunteers, or bystanders asked about our religion or faith, we responded honestly from our faith experience. And they asked many questions regarding God, faith, and suffering.

Many workers, volunteers, or visitors to Ground Zero either had no religious backgrounds or only retained piecemealed bits of knowledge recalled from Sunday school lessons learned as a child. Some considered themselves Christians because they were good people who offered kindness and help to those in need.

But now with the terrorist attacks, the destruction of major national landmarks, and the loss of so many lives, people started wondering and asking, "What's my purpose in life?" And they questioned chaplains about eternity.

When asked about my faith, I answered: "I know, without a doubt, I'm going to heaven when my time on earth comes to an end. That knowledge and assurance helps me cope with difficulties and sorrows here on earth. My temporary problems here pale beside my promise of an eternal afterlife with God."

"How do you know?" they asked. "How can you be so sure?"

With this opening, I offered a brief personal testimony and my belief that God has a purpose for each of our lives.

I admitted I'd not always been so strong in my faith. Raised in a Catholic home, I attended church on Sundays, but after I graduated from high school and left home for military life, I dropped my religious background for a more carefree approach to life. In my twenties I returned to Christianity and realized that salvation guarantees the hope of heaven. When we live out Christ's commands—serving others, caring for those in need, and feeding the hungry—good works follow faith.

But, at times, differences in chaplains' theological interpretations created misunderstandings at Ground Zero. On one occasion, I worked with a older chaplain who appeared quiet and withdrawn. Exhausted, he still worked like a trooper. His stamina, wisdom, and no-nonsense approach exemplified how seriously he took his job.

After one recovery, he placed the human tissue remains in a special container. I asked, "Do you want to pray?"

"I don't pray for dead people."

"I don't pray for dead people, either. I want to pray that this particular person is identified by their DNA for their family's sake."

He walked away without responding, and we didn't have the opportunity to speak to one another after that occasion. This chaplain's wisdom resounded in a way that never left me. I often wish I could thank this chaplain for his candor.

Thankful for this chaplain's example, after that, I was careful to be clear about my intentions for prayer: to thank God for the gift of each person's life and the blessing each individual was for their family, and then to pray for comfort for the grieving family.

The Apostle Paul's prayer in Philippians 1:3-5 reminds me of the quiet lesson I learned from him: *"I thank my God in all my remembrance of you, always offering prayer with joy in my every prayer for you all, in view of your participation in the gospel from the first day until now."*

42

Exhausted Lord, But Ready

"Quietly . . . softly, God taps on our tense shoulders with His love."

—Shawntel Jefferson

I completed five tours of duty of various time lengths. Like other chaplains and volunteers, I rotated in and out based on my responsibilities at home and the time available to get away from work. But during my fifth tour, I sensed my emotional margin drew near to my stress limit.

One afternoon, I sat in the chapel, exhausted and in desperate need of rest, relaxation, and time away from the emotional demands of working with the search and recovery crews. A St. Paul's volunteer approached me and said, "Someone donated tickets to the play *Music Man*. Would you like to go?"

Still in my firefighter's turnout gear, I asked, "Are you serious? Yeah, I'd love to go, but I can't go dressed like this."

"Yes, I'm serious, and it doesn't matter how you're dressed."

Thoughts scrambled through my head. *I don't know my way around New York City. How will I get to the theater? And get back?* "I don't know how to get there."

"No problem. I know someone who'll give you a ride."

The volunteer led me to a well-groomed, elegant-looking woman who introduced herself as Lesley Visser. Lesley's manner of dress certainly didn't fit in with the typical turnout gear, shabby jeans, or heavy coveralls of Ground Zero—and none too clean at that. I had no idea who this woman was, but she was larger-than-life, down-to-earth, and friendly. She shook my hand and invited me to join her for the trip to the theater.

We went outside the chapel, and lo and behold, a shiny black stretch limousine waited at the curb. *Whoa. Who goes for rides in limousines? And from Ground Zero. Who is this woman?*

We enjoyed the musical but didn't stay for the whole show; Lesley's cell phone kept ringing. After we left, we sat down for a little and talked about our families.

Sitting in a coffee shop, she talked to me as if we were old friends. This interaction transported me to a different place far from the twisted rubble and dirty faces of the Pile.

Then she received a call from CBS. They needed her.

Whoa, CBS?

Lesley's limousine driver drove us to CBS studios where she led me on a fascinating behind-the-scenes tour. Then she showed me an interview she conducted with Doug Flutie, a NFL quarterback.

Lesley asked, "Do you know who Doug Flutie threw his first TD pass to?"

Ha. I'm a Chicago Bears fan. Of course I know. "Walter Peyton, running back for Chicago Bears."

She seemed surprised and pleased I answered her question.

Everyone at CBS recognized Lesley and tried to anticipate her every need. People checked with her in a very professional manner. A thought flipped through my mind. *Okay, she is one important woman in this organization.*

Turns out, she was a famous sportscaster with CBS and the first female NFL analyst on TV. The only woman inducted into the Football Hall of Fame chauffeured me—a grubby-looking chaplain—around New York City in a sleek black limousine.

Afterwards, we headed back to St. Paul's in the limo, and Lesley called her mother on the phone. "I just took a Ground Zero chaplain to a play on Broadway." She seemed as proud of me as I was of her.

Lesley's mother asked to talk to me. She and I talked together for about twenty minutes. I was so touched by our conversation; it seemed like talking to my sweet mother.

As we spoke on the phone, Lesley's mother asked me about Jesus and heaven. "I want to be sure I'm going to heaven," she said.

I was impressed by how quickly we arrived at that point in our conversation, especially since she was already well versed on where she needed to be in her spiritual walk. She told me she understood she was a sinner and had asked God for forgiveness. She was familiar with the whole Bible story of Jesus: that He died on the cross, was buried, and rose again on the third day.

"Do you know Jesus Christ as your personal savior?"

"Yes."

"Do you know John 3:16?"

"Yes." And we recited it together: *"For God so loved the world, that He gave His only begotten Son, that whoever believes in Him shall not perish, but have eternal life."*

This fine lady loved the Gospel message and the story of salvation, and she wanted me to pray with her.

I asked her to repeat after me: "Lord Jesus, I'm a sinner, and I know it. I know I cannot save myself, and I want to ask you into my heart to be my personal Lord and Savior."

We prayed and talked together over the phone a bit more, and then said our goodbyes. She wished me well in my work at Ground Zero.

Lesley's mother radiated godly reverence. I was so proud of her for praying with me over the phone. As we talked, I heard comfort and relief in her voice.

The evening surpassed my wildest expectations. The adventure and the company lifted my mental and emotional fatigue, and the loving interaction with Lesley's mother rejuvenated me.

Thank you, Lesley, for taking the time to minister to a chaplain in need of uplifting. *And thank You, Lord, for bringing this lovely woman into my life when I needed encouragement and redirection.*

Yes, Lesley and her mother's thoughtful interaction reinforced my calling: to comfort heartbroken individuals and to help others with their spiritual needs and bring them into God's sheepfold.

43

My Self-Pity Party

"It is natural for us to wish that God had designed for us a less glorious and less arduous destiny; but then we are wishing not for more love but for less."

—C. S. Lewis

One December night near the end of my last tour at Ground Zero, I walked alone on the Pile, trying to stay warm. By now, searchers found fewer remains in the shrinking Pile, and chaplains performed fewer memorial tributes. A number of chaplains returned to their families and livelihoods, but I remained in Manhattan. Cold and exhausted, I wanted to go home.

I sat down in the dark shadows off to the side of the debris pile and waited in case any searchers found human remains. Surrounded by teams of workers scurrying all over the Pile in that Hollywood lighting, I felt alone. The cold night air slapped me in the face and brought me back to reality, forcing me to examine my attitude. Instead of leaning into God, I wallowed in my misery.

I challenged God. *Why did You bring me back to this miserable place? My chaplain friends have returned home to their families for restoration. What do You want me to do now that things are under better control and workers are making fewer recoveries? Why am I still here?*

I missed my loving wife. I missed my sweet children. I missed my warm home. I even missed my old teasing buddies back at the Chicago fire station.

I looked all around me and observed the swarms of workers still committing time and energy to clean up Ground Zero, and to get New York City back on its feet. I realized the suffering continued, and God's compassion must still be shared.

I sobered up quickly and stopped feeling sorry for myself. I prayed for God's comforting presence and recalled warm thoughts of my family and better times. I meditated on Scripture: *"Finally, brethren, whatever is true, whatever is honorable, whatever is right, whatever is pure, whatever is lovely, whatever is of good repute, if there is any excellence and if anything worthy of praise, dwell on these things."* (Philippians 4:8)

I sang *Amazing Grace*, a song written over two hundred years ago by John Newton in a small town in England. The words and phrases, familiar to so many, fit this time and place and comforted me. The song reminded me of the world's temporary nature and the need to keep my focus on the eternal. We live in a speck of time, but eternity with God is forever.

Amazing grace! How sweet the sound/That saved a wretch like me!
Through many dangers, toils, and snares,/I have already come;
'Tis grace hath brought me safe thus far,/And grace will lead me home.
When we've been there ten thousand years,/Bright shining as the sun
We've no less days to sing God's praise/Than when we'd first begun.

Praying, singing, and meditating on God's love and on eternity moved me to a better place emotionally and spiritually, away from my pitiful, selfish whining. Refreshed and energized again, I started to walk the perimeter, ready to offer encouragement to others.

Minutes later, I met up with a paramedic deep in the same melancholy I'd felt earlier. He, too, was away from his family and his children, and he missed them. This man lost close friends in the attacks on the World Trade Center, and he grieved for them. Seeing this destruction day after day forced him to imagine how his friends died, adding to his pain.

"Why does one person live and the other die?" He asked.

Survivor's guilt, a common theme among these workers, dominated his thinking. "I keep searching the towers' debris field, almost subconsciously, looking for bits of human tissue or pieces of clothing and equipment among the downed beams and girders. But I'll never find my friends. This destruction is too massive. Their remains so small in comparison. How can I go on without them? They were such an important part of my everyday life."

The harsh reality of the loss of his friends who perished hit him hard over and over again. This paramedic suffered devastating, permanent losses of his buddies in the worst way imaginable. Only those with similar experiences comprehended the burden this man shouldered every day.

Compared to his brokenness, missing my family, my friends, and my stable life back home seemed minimal. After all, my loneliness and exhaustion of serving on the Pile only temporarily inconvenienced me. My wife and children, a few hours away by plane, would soon welcome me home.

We talked a long time, and I prayed with him. His willingness to talk about his friends' deaths showed courage, which humbled me. Our one-time counseling session was not enough to ease his ongoing deepseated sorrow. I held out hope for his future and encouraged him to seek follow-up counseling.

As I reflected on my time with this paramedic, I talked to God: *Thank You, Lord, for answering my prayer, for pulling me out of my selfish pit of despondency, and directing me to share Your glory with someone suffering emotional agony. Thank You for showing me that my problems are temporary and for reminding me to keep my eyes on eternity. "You are awesome, O God, in Your sanctuary." You give power and strength to Your people. Praise be to God. Please guide my paramedic friend to seek follow-up counseling. Cover him with angel's wings and protect his mind and health. In Your name, I pray. Amen.*

44

Holding Myself Together

"The heart is a strange beast and not ruled by logic."

—Maria V. Snyder

In my travels, friends and work associates asked many times, "How did you handle what you saw and heard at Ground Zero?"

Frankly, I wished for a switch to turn my emotions on and off. In ministry, my emotions never shut down. Maybe that's what troubled me. Overwhelmed, I was unprepared for the magnitude of the devastation I observed, and the traumatic stories I listened to day after day that I can't fully express in words.

It's like the proverbial man who gives you a measuring cup and says, "Bail all the water out of Lake Michigan, and I'll give you a million dollars." The hardship is such an incomprehensible impossibility that you just hand the cup back and walk away. Sometimes being present to comfort people in disaster situations seems like that. To protect my mental health, I worked hard to keep other people's emotional heartache in perspective, but I was not always successful.

I hurt deeply within for those who suffered losses at Ground Zero. Even today deep sorrow overwhelms me for people who lose loved ones, who suffer chronic or terminal illness, who struggle with broken relationships, who struggle with addiction, or battle life in other ways.

There is no on-off button for me to push. The only electrician who understands me is God. Thankfully, he knows I'm a work-in-progress. My circuitry overloaded more than once at the Pile. I wanted to be an excellent Christian example for others, but I fell shamelessly short at times. I was a sinner with faults, and at times, I failed. But I asked God for strength, and He provided encouragement and support.

Second to God, my family held me together. They supported me after each return home from Ground Zero. Sue, my daughters, and I always visited my mom's house first, where I shared bits of what I experienced. I never shared complete details of Ground Zero's unimaginable devastation and the brokenness of the people in New York City.

My brother, Steve, told me of my mother's pride in me. My mom, my wife, my sisters, Anne Marie and Linda, my brother, Steve, and my daughters all surrounded me and loved me. Their care made this human tragedy at least a bit more manageable.

Whenever I traveled to New York City, my mother worried, as mothers do. To lesson her fears, I called her right from the center of the

Pile during brief work stoppages to say, "Hi." Hearing her voice proved equally soothing for me.

Her questions made me smile. "Are you eating enough?" "Are you getting enough rest?" She prayed for me every day, and I felt her prayer support all the time. I gave her a picture taken of me on the perimeter at Ground Zero, which she placed on the mantle where it sits to this day.

My gentle wife, Sue, and I engaged in deep discussions about what transpired in New York City. Radiating understanding, she just let me talk. Occasionally she coaxed out thoughts or ideas or memories.

My wife and I both understood the time apart and the consequences of missing each other. One day, I desperately missed my wife and just wanted talk with her, but I was working on the Pile. The noise and confusion of clean-up activities prevented me from calling to catch up with the current issues at home. I just released it to the Lord, and within a few minutes, my wife called me on my cell phone to tell me how much she loved and missed me.

Despite the noise, when I spoke with her I heard her voice just fine. I could hardly contain my excitement. Like an electrical switch that shuts off to prevent damage from an electrical overload, this brief conversation reset my emotional circuit breaker with enough current to continue serving others on the Pile that day.

God knows how He wired me, and He also knows how just how much my emotional circuits can tolerate. My wife also sensed when my emotional circuits were strained to the limit. Our conversations helped to lower my sensory overload.

I'm thankful for my sweet wife who Proverbs 31:10-12 describes: *"An excellent wife, who can find? For her worth is far above jewels. The heart of her husband trusts in her, and he will have no lack of gain. She does him good and not evil all the days of her life."*

45

I'm Done: My Last Night at Ground Zero

"Memories warm you up from the inside. But they also tear you apart."

—Haruki Murakami

On my last night of my last tour of duty in New York City, I sat right at the edge of the Tower 2 rubble pile and prayed for an hour or more. This was the final time I'd pray at the Pile. I reflected on all the people I'd come to love and honor here in this spiritual place. As I thought about saying goodbye to my Ground Zero flock, my tears flowed. I asked God to bless all of them—my coworkers on the Pile, the chaplains with whom I shared my deepest hurts, the staff members at St. Paul's Chapel, the firefighters, the police officers, the construction workers, the volunteers, and the families and friends who lost loved ones.

I sensed God's presence, Who dwelled here in the air and in the soil. Many of His children died here. I'd conducted many funerals, hugged suffering folks, talked to hurting people, and received blessings from those around me. A part of my soul now rested in Ground Zero. I'd never be the same again.

Oh yes, I was still Bob Ossler, but a much more sensitive man. Broken in attitude, more forgiving, slower to judge, and gentler in my newer spiritual approach to people. God softened my heart. I listened to heroes whose hearts were filled with pain and to people troubled by vivid memories and horrendous recollections. These memories were not the kind to share with families and children. Even if they or I could articulate these disturbing experiences, who wanted to hear about or envision the atrocities we witnessed and handled? The absolute magnitude of evil and terror that struck Manhattan on September 11, 2001, remained seared in our memories until death do we part.

As I sat, I looked over all of Ground Zero, I recalled the debris I touched, the places where I crouched with people to pray, and the places where I helped search for remains. Each crag and chasm and chamber of Ground Zero stored a memory for me. Sitting there on the Pile that last night, I still smelled death. I still saw and heard the clean-up going on. I still tasted the grit in the air and felt the earth rumbling all around.

I recognized my time was up, and soon I'd leave to go home to my loved ones. I'd never see these people again. The empty feeling of impending loss hit me hard. Even so, my heart and mind stored my memories of those I'd never see again this side of heaven.

46

Home at Last

"Everybody has to leave, everybody has to leave their home and come back so they can love it again for all new reasons."

—Donald Miller

Returning home from Ground Zero for the last time sparked heartache. I felt like a pastor abandoning his flock with no hope of returning. Saying goodbye and admitting I might never see all those workers and volunteers who converged at Ground Zero from so many different places was difficult. I ached for my Ground Zero friends. We'd cried together, read Scripture together, prayed together, and held onto each other. We'd shared our intimate family stories and confided our fears. We'd bonded as one big family on the Pile, but now these family members dispersed, to go their own ways, back to their lives and families.

I wrote these words in the front of my Ground Zero Bible, the Bible I carried with me every moment I walked the perimeter or the Pile: *"May I always remember that I can lay my burdens down at the Lord's cross. I leave this place with a sense of finished work, as a child of God serving other children of God. What an honor to have served my almighty God in such a way. I leave here longing for Sue and the girls, Noelle, Michelle, and Heather. I pray that I may serve my family just a little better through this experience. I think I understand the pain a pastor must feel when leaving a congregation. It hurts to say goodbye to my flock."*

The words of David in Psalm 5:1-4, 11-12 captured my feelings: *"Give ear to my words, O Lord, consider my groaning. Heed the sound of my cry for help, my King and my God, for to You I pray. In the morning, O Lord, You will hear my voice; in the morning I will order my prayer to You and eagerly watch. For You are not a God who takes pleasure in wickedness; no evil dwells with You. But let all who take refuge in You be glad, let them ever sing for joy; and may You shelter them, that those who love Your name may exult in You. For it is You who blesses the righteous man, O Lord, You surround him with favor as with a shield."*

Already missing these special friends in New York City, I prayed and mourned the whole flight home.

When I walked in the door of my home and reunited with my family, their joy at seeing me lifted my spirits. They all grabbed onto me and just loved me. After a bit, I relaxed in a long hot shower. The comfort and joy of being home juxtaposed with the devastation and sorrow I'd left behind in Manhattan proved too much to handle. As I stood in the shower, I sobbed uncontrollably. I felt like a shaking, blithering idiot. My wife heard my weeping and ran into the shower. She held me and consoled me with her tender words.

The crushing sadness and emotional pain I'd suppressed for so long finally erupted. Sue soothed the profound sorrow and emotional distress overwhelming me. She tenderly held me and talked softly reassuring me, "Everything will be all right." I felt my darling wife's full trust and love. I trusted and believed her because she'd never, ever let me down.

Finally, I calmed down. Although I occasionally broke down in tears when answering questions about Ground Zero, I never again melted down like that.

SECTION 10

Comforter of Our Significant Sorrow

"But the God who loves you is master of your significant sorrow. He calls you to go through even this hard thing. Though it feels impossible and devastates earthly hopes, He sets a boundary (not where we'd set it). He convinces you that this hard thing will come out good beyond all you can ask, imagine, see, hear, or conceive in your heart." (Ephesians 3:20; 1 Corinthians 2:9)

—David Powlison

47

Finding God's Message in the Wreckage

"God loves each of us as if there were only one of us."

—St. Augustine

As fireballs and smoke blew out of the Twin Towers, questions flew out of the lips of many who witnessed human cruelty unfold, burning people into ashes. No sooner had the Twin Towers collapsed into wild chaos than questions flared up from the smoke and ashes of the Pile. *"Where was God?" "Can I still believe in God?" "How can such an evil act be done in the name of God?" "What kind of God allows this?"*

When terrorism and man's inhumanity against man murders time again and again, three words epitomize the questions tormenting our wounded souls—religion, relationship, and retaliation.

The human passion of intolerant religiosity mobilized the destructive force of monstrous evil. Nineteen terrorists hijackers planned and willfully murdered thousands, and the force of evil invaded our national psyche. The New Testament calls the forces of evil as *"principalities* (of demons) *and powers* (the liberty to do as one pleases)." (Ephesians 1:21) Detached from God, evil took residence in the emptiness of murderers who maimed, killed, and destroyed.

159

In the tragic dramas of life, connection and relationship with God erases boundaries—between enemy and friend, between life and death—and connects us to His love. In Jesus' most famous sermon, the Sermon on the Mount, He said, *"You have heard that it was said, 'You shall love your neighbor and hate your enemy.' But I say to you, love your enemies and pray for those who persecute you."* (Matthew 5:43-44)

Jesus also summed up God's message to the world: *"And you shall love the Lord your God with all your heart, and with all your soul, and with all your mind, and with all your strength.' The second is this, 'You shall love your neighbor as yourself.' There is no other commandment greater than these."* (Mark 12:30-31; Leviticus 19:18)

Trapped in the window of terrorism's death, a man and woman reached out to each other. Connected in life, they stepped into space, hand in hand, staying connected until they entered eternity. The final phone calls of those trapped in the towers connected one last time with loved ones to say, "I love you."

September 11th's dark night of the soul catapulted many into spiritual crisis. When life isn't fair, suffering tests our trust in God Who is just. Vengeance and retaliation demands, *"Where is the God of justice, the avenger of evil?"*

The cleansing power of God's raw, naked love in the face of lawlessness declares, "I love you." The fire of forging a relationship with God—that link to absolute love—energizes the constructive source of love, grace, comfort, and peace.

God's love isn't a spectator sport. I joined the fray of salvage and salvation and witnessed God onsite, at work in the faces and actions of workers and volunteers in that hallowed, open-air cathedral—Ground Zero. Mourning with those who mourned, we confronted tragedy head-on and forged an intense camaraderie.

On March 30, 2002 a firefighter discovered the fragile pages of a Bible fused onto a heart-shaped piece of melted steel that now resides in the 9/11 Memorial and Museum in Manhattan. God's Word and a sobering message from the Sermon on the Mount survived the fire, horror, and tangled rubble of 9/11.

Just as Jesus' message of love and peace has outlasted wars, persecution, and trials throughout the centuries. Just as the heart and soul of God's love was fused onto heart-shaped steel, the fragility of faith tempered by tragedy can survive and remain fused on our hearts.

Out of over 700,000 words in the Bible, what message withstood the devastation of 9/11? *"Ye have heard that it hath been said, An eye for an eye, and a tooth for a tooth: But I say unto you, That ye resist not evil: but whosoever shall smite thee on thy right cheek, turn to him the other also."* (Matthew 5:38-49)

48

Where Was God?

*"Poor God, how often He is blamed for all the suffering in the world.
It's like praising Satan for allowing all the good that happens."*

—E. A. Bucchianeri

After the attacks, many people demanded to know, "Where was God when the twin towers fell?"

Reverend Lyndon Harris, the priest who transformed his church into a refuge for first responders addressed the question: "My sense is that God was right there, and that the first heart to break on 9/11 was the heart of God, because people with free will chose to do evil things, and that's the price we pay for the world we have."

When faced with the reality of evil, Mother Teresa pointed out how God works through ordinary people. "There is a light in this world, a healing spirit more powerful than any darkness we may encounter. We sometimes lose sight of this force when there is suffering, too much pain. Then suddenly, the spirit will emerge through the lives of ordinary people who hear a call and answer in extraordinary ways."

And Billy Graham added this thought on the issue. "We are reminded of the mystery of reality of evil. I have been asked hundreds of times why God allows tragedy and suffering. I have to confess that I do not know the answer. I have to accept, by faith, that God is sovereign and that He is a God of love and mercy and compassion in the midst of suffering."

In New York City, I witnessed the harsh reality of evil, but I also saw the spirit of God working through ordinary people in extraordinary circumstances. I'm not sure I can ever reach down deep enough inside of me to explain the kind of spiritual experience being at Ground Zero was for me. It wasn't an epiphany or a religious conversion. I'm also not saying I possess a better understanding or am more spiritual than anyone else who worked or volunteered there. That would be naïve. As I counseled with those suffering with the loss of loved ones, I felt God's presence with me.

On the ground in Manhattan, individuals of every faith helped one another. Everywhere I turned I saw well-oiled teams firing on all cylinders, steadily working to get the clean-up job done. September 11th was a devastating historical moment in time, and people of New York City and others from around the country stepped up to help. They held a deep powerful respect for those who died and for this city struggling to get back on its feet. It didn't matter which faith group they belonged to, or even if they didn't belong to one at all.

Skeptics and believers alike asked, "Where was God on 9/11?"

The simple answer is: "God was there."

When all you can see is evil's hand, trust God's heart. Look what happened at Ground Zero when God touched hearts. Just as Jesus provided the fine wine at the wedding feast in the Bible. Just as He multiplied the loaves and fishes for hungry families after giving His most famous sermon, God supplied food and water for thousands of workers and volunteers.

He used the hands and hearts of His faithful followers, regardless of primary religious beliefs, to carry out His mission to soothe the broken-hearted and feed the hungry. Every day while on my tours at Ground Zero, I walked past cartons of donated water, Gatorade, carbonated drinks, Granola bars, and other assorted consumables piled high on the sidewalk. Restaurants brought food to tired and hungry workers and volunteers. Other organizations provided food, housing, and emotional support. Even the downtown Dunkin' Donuts graciously gave free coffee to exhausted workers.

Volunteers by the dozens stood by to serve and care for those who worked tirelessly around the clock at Ground Zero. These volunteers, many from great distances, gave their time and money to help New York City recover.

Where was God? Right there in the hands and hearts of these workers and volunteers.

After my experiences in Manhattan, I saw my fellow man in a much better light, and I thank God every day for their loving, human kindness, and their determination to move forward in life.

Ministering at Ground Zero catapulted me to a higher spiritual level and plunged me to my knees like never before. I constantly prayed, asking God to intervene in every situation, no matter how big or small, in a constant open dialogue. My reliance on God was deep and special. When you walk in the Spirit, life looks better, and the joy you feel is stronger.

49

Triumph Over Terror

"He had just helped pull three bodies from the rubble when he saw it there in dawn's first light, standing in a sea of debris. A heavenly symbol in a hellish setting. A cross. Exhausted and traumatized by his labors, the man dropped to his knees in tears. 'It was a sign,' Frank Silecchia would recall, 'a sign that God hadn't deserted us.'"

—*USA Today*, May 15, 2014

"You have to see the House of God. You won't believe what you'll see," another chaplain said to me as I prayer-walked the perimeter.

The House of God? In the rubble of the gates of hell? What was he talking about?

He led me toward an edge of the Pile where the partially collapsed 6 World Trade Center remained. We passed through a breach in the destruction and negotiated our steps over the rubble. Work continued around the Pile and the vibration of these damaged structures rumbled under our feet. Bursts of ash from partially standing upper floors fell sporadically.

I felt uneasy about being in this spot, but also compelled to see what the chaplain meant. He stopped and pointed upward. A section of wall, still standing, rose beside us. On the dirty surface, someone spray-painted in giant letters "The House of God." An arrow pointed us deeper into the rubble of this apocalypse.

As we walked further in, we saw layers of concrete floors collapsed like stacks of pancakes. Sections of wall, half-fallen, blocked our path. Crushed beams and bent girders, torn and twisted like flimsy aluminum foil, littered the scene. Rays of sunlight broke through the shattered building, lighting up the scene before me like a Norman Rockwell painting. In the middle of the dust-filled air, two steel beams intersected forming the shape of a cross. Impaled in the rubble at a vertical angle, the cross stretched up from the purgatory of suffering, the burning pit where souls had been lost.

I looked around and spotted a number of smaller steel beam crosses on the Pile. No human cut these crosses or planted them upright in the debris, but there they stood, like a message from God: *Remember this. Even in the aftermath of evil's nightmare, My love flows for you. My mercy and compassion outstrips terror and death.*

Frank Silecchia, a construction worker, explored caverns in the Pile looking for possible survivors and discovered a 17-foot tall cross on September 13, 2001. Silecchia alerted Father Brian Jordan, a Franciscan friar who committed to saving this large cross for others to see. Because of the precarious nature of its original setting and the need to clean up the 16-acre hellscape, engineers moved the cross to a temporary location on West Street for everyone to see.

The Ground Zero Cross now stands on display in the National September 11th Memorial and Museum on the site of the original Twin Towers. Many who saw the cross in its original location hailed it as an important symbol of faith.

For me, this cross, a miracle rising from the rubble of hell, was proof to me that the tenderness of God overcomes evil. God left His signature—a 4000 pound, 17-foot-long steel crossbeam, rising in triumph from terror's hellish wasteland.

5 0

Moving Forward after Tragedy

"There is no pit so deep, that God's love is not deeper still."

—Corrie ten Boom

Writing these pages stirred up memories that overwhelmed me. Here I am, fifteen years after the attacks of September 11th, and I feel like I just left the Pile hours ago. All those thoughts and feelings from Ground Zero flooded back. One memory led to another memory, transporting me right back to the noise, the putrid air, the grit in my mouth, the unending sorrow.

When people say, "Wow, you've been to Ground Zero. That's so interesting. What was it like?"

How can I explain? Oh, yes, I cherish good memories of friends made and hearts touched, but they're buried among graphic, ominous, spirit-crushing sights: mangled bodies, decomposing pieces of someone's loved one, putrefying flesh mixed with smells of burnt jet fuel, heat, cold and physical exhaustion, glaring lights turning night into day, the ceaseless cacophony of machine noises, and sobs issuing from shattered human hearts.

I'd gladly trade my experiences at Ground Zero for a chance to bring all those lovely people back to life and back to their families.

Yes, that's an impossible dream, but I live with these painful memories that will never leave me. How many Ground Zero heroes still suffer from their losses? How many feel their noses rubbed into the agony every time a misguided terrorist kills innocent victims? And how many suffer today with either depression or physical illnesses caused by exposure to toxic fumes and dust-filled air? How many endure respiratory illnesses? How many contracted cancer? How many have already died?

At Ground Zero, I observed in amazement the depth of human suffering and how people dealt with their pain day in and day out. I saw emotions from opposite ends of the spectrum: from people catatonic with fear to those with superhuman strength and resilience.

I wondered, *Will those who suffer so deeply ever be okay?*

I, too, felt numb at times and just wanted to leave that terrible mess behind, go home and hold my wife and children. The work challenged my mental health, but God protected me. He's been my rock and my salvation. I looked back and realized I'd reached the bottom of my pit emotionally, which rattles me still today.

No training, no school, no book, no expert ever taught me how to prepare for the magnitude of Ground Zero. I never told my wife or my young children everything I experienced in New York City. I insulated my family from most of what happened, which isolated me from them for many years.

My experience serving on the Pile transformed me into a person who can read feelings almost like a lie detector. Because of my pain, my sensitivity level detects pain in others.

But hitting the bottom of that pit was not the end. From the pit, I climbed back up by trusting in the Lord. I grew stronger, if not a little too sensitive. Even though God never left my side, at times, I felt abandoned by people. Oh, I don't mean my wife or kids or even my closest friends who provided wonderful support.

Unable to bear hearing Ground Zero stories, one of the nicest people I've ever known became cold and distant toward me. My friend's attitude stunned me. However, his reaction, too, was perfectly normal.

Normal reactions to abnormal situations scare some people. Those who experience trauma get better when they talk about it. Others with secondary connections sometimes can't bear to listen to the stories, so they distance themselves. Everyone responds differently, and that's normal.

At times when I shared a story, the intensity of the mental turmoil reactivated powerful emotions. I'd be fine in life at home for a while, but then I'd receive a call to go back to New York City to help, triggering a relapse into memories. Through time and prayer this anxiety went away, and I found relief.

A writer friend, who is both a psychologist and member of our local monthly writers' critique group, listened as I read a Ground Zero story written for this book. Reading my account, fifteen years after the events, propelled me right back onto that stinking jumbled pile of rubbish and human misery. I saw the faces. I heard the noise. I smelled the awful odors. Intense emotional pain overwhelmed me. I lost my composure and started to cry. Everyone in the group remained respectfully quiet and gave me time to compose myself. After I regained control and finished the story, my friend said, "That was intense. If you ever want to talk, I'm here, brother."

Bringing up these stories triggered more emotional turmoil than I wanted or expected. I now realized why I wondered. *Should I ever write or tell these stories of workers, volunteers, and chaplains at the Pile?*

As I wrote out these memories, I felt vulnerable. As I recalled them, the sharp physical and emotional pain I experienced surged back. By the grace of God, my head was clear. I didn't feel like I had to "man up" or be brave and strong or not show weakness. I'm weak. I admit that. I'm sensitive and sometimes thin-skinned, but I've come a long way.

Vulnerability prompted feelings of helplessness and now that the truth is out, I feel better. Terror has not triumphed over me, because I know I can rely on my God.

I've triumphed over terror. In all circumstances, I rely on these biblical admonitions. *"Rejoice always; pray without ceasing; in everything give thanks; for this is God's will for you in Christ Jesus."* (1 Thessalonians 5:16-18)

51

Finding Purpose Again

"Know the purpose of life that you are drawn to. Do what makes your heart leap rather than simply follow some style or fashion."

—Jonas Salk

As I reflected on my time at Ground Zero, a different void surfaced in my life. The majority of my working life I'd rescued people in physical distress, escorted them to hospitals, saved them from burning buildings, or pulled them from the waters of Lake Michigan. But at Ground Zero, I ministered at a deeper emotional and spiritual level to individuals in profound distress.

At home, the feeling of missing my Ground Zero flock intensified. So I decided to put my theological training into practice and find a church that needed a pastor. I wanted to continue ministering to people who yearned to know God and longed for spiritual growth. I felt God calling me into His service.

After I settled down and got back into the swing of things at home and work, I shared this calling with my wife. Now my sweet wife is not your everyday, outgoing pastor's wife. She's friendly, loving, and has an impressive background. But the idea of being a pastor's wife took her by surprise. Even so, she said, "Okay, Bob. Let's give it a try. If God wants that to happen, He will prepare the way and remove any obstacles."

I researched all over the Chicago area and found a small church in Sauk Village, Illinois that was looking for a pastor. This church was about an hour-and-a-half drive each way from my home. For my first interview, I drove through a snowstorm to interview with Ron McClain, a church elder. The meeting felt like ordination all over again with thorough questioning of my beliefs and knowledge of the Bible. I loved every second of the interview.

Later I met with the search committee who invited me to preach on several Sundays and to meet the church members. It may have been a tiny congregation and a small church, but to me it was a cathedral. Bursting with energy and excitement, I couldn't wait to preach about Jesus. I prayed so hard about becoming the pastor of this church that I think God wanted to shut me up.

After giving a few Sunday sermons, the search committee hired me, and I became a bi-vocational pastor, working full-time for the Chicago Fire Department and part-time for the church. Let me tell you here and now, there's no such thing as a part-time pastor. I was on the clock every minute. I was always visiting, always calling, always going somewhere for a person in need. Pastoring was the hardest work I've ever done in my life, and I loved serving.

Before being hired, I vowed to the search team that I'd go door to door to visit every person in the community, and I managed to cover about ninety percent of that town while pastoring the church over several years. The church grew and people matured in their personal relationship with Jesus Christ.

When I retired from full-time work with the Chicago Fire Department in February of 2006 and moved to Arizona. Sauk Village Bible Church was going strong with approximately 140 people attending. I miss those Sauk Village people and keep them in my prayers. My heart and mind store precious memories of my flock.

52

Honoring the Fallen
343 Pairs of Boots

"Faith all grown up is trust."

—Adam LiVecchi

When I moved to Mayer, Arizona, I served as pastor at Mayer Community Church and also volunteered as chaplain with the Mayer Fire Department under Chief Glen Brown.

Over the years, Ground Zero remained embedded in my mind and heart. Whenever anyone asked, I spoke at community events about Ground Zero and American heroism. Ingrained in my soul and my memories, my time spent serving on the Pile contributes to my actions and choices in life.

Every September, Americans in cities around the country remember the 9/11 attacks with ceremonies, speeches, parades, and special displays. Since 2002, The Healing Fields, a dramatic display of 3000 flags, one for each person who lost their life in the terrorist attacks, commemorates the victims killed on 9/11. To date, over 500 of these Healing Fields events have been organized around the country. A sobering and moving display of patriotism and honor to those killed, the Healing Fields touch the hearts of national and international visitors alike. A person cannot visit one of these displays without feeling the sobering impact of the devastating loss of so many people.

Prescott Valley, Arizona Councilwoman Mary Mallory organized the first Prescott Valley Healing Fields of Northern Arizona in 2012. Two years later, I joined the planning meeting for the annual event. The committee wanted to place a pair of firefighter boots next to each flag dedicated to the firefighters killed on 9/11. But how would it possible to secure 343 pairs of firefighter boots within the short timeline before the scheduled event?

I thought, *Why not? We can do this.* I volunteered to obtain the boots.

After the meeting, someone on the committee approached me. "Haven't you bitten off more than you can chew?" But I remembered how God answered my prayers at Ground Zero for crosses and candles. If God provided those crosses for workers on the Pile and those candles for St. Paul's Chapel, then He'd certainly help us find 343 pairs of firefighter boots.

With the help of a friend of the committee, Kirk Mallory, we accomplished the almost-impossible. After hundreds of emails, uncounted phone calls, numerous miles of travel, and many UPS deliveries, we surpassed our boot count goal.

What an inspiration to see all those boots with the designated flags for the lost firefighters. I made it a point to touch every flag on display and pray for each family and their loved ones. God bless the firefighters, police officers, and emergency responders who died serving our country, and the civilians who died with them. Rest in peace, my friends.

Sometimes we pray and ask God for what seems impossible. Then when we receive it, we're surprised. A little section in Ephesians 3:14-21 reminds of us the power of prayer *"I [Paul, an Apostle of Jesus Christ] bow my knees before the Father, from whom every family in heaven and on earth derives its name, that He would grant you, according to the riches of His glory, to be strengthened with power through His Spirit in the inner man, so that Christ may dwell in your hearts through faith; and that you, being rooted and grounded in love, may be able to comprehend with all the saints what is the breadth and length and height and depth, and to know the love of Christ which surpasses knowledge, that you may be filled up to all the fullness of God. Now to Him who is able to do far more abundantly beyond all that we ask or think, according to the power that works within us, to Him be the glory in the church and in Christ Jesus to all generations forever and ever. Amen."*

52

Closing the Circle

"The most beautiful people we have known are those who have known defeat, known suffering, known struggle, known loss, and have found their way out of the depths. These persons have an appreciation, a sensitivity and an understanding of life that fills them with compassion, gentleness, and a deep loving concern."

—Elizabeth Kubler-Ross

On September 12, 2001, I accepted the challenge thrown my way: "Hey Bob, did you hear the news? New York City authorities need chaplains at Ground Zero. You gonna go?"

I'm amazed how God combined my training and talents in ways I never imagined. Over the years, firefighting and paramedic emergency services, chaplaincy training, and ordination answered and confirmed the calling as described in 1 Peter 5:2-4: *"Be shepherds of God's flock that is under your care, serving as overseers—not because you must, but because you are willing, as God wants you to be; not greedy for money, but eager to serve; not lording it over those entrusted to you, but being examples to the flock. And when the Chief Shepherd appears, you will receive the crown of glory that will never fade away."*

About the Authors

"You may encounter many defeats, but you must not be defeated. In fact, it may be necessary to encounter the defeats, so you can know who you are, what you can rise from, how you can still come out of it."

—Maya Angelou

Bob Ossler is no stranger to personal trials. From an early age, he watched his mother, a single parent, struggle to support his two older sisters and his younger brother. The pain of his father's abandonment of their family erupted in school where he acted out. By age 11, his mother remarried, and his new dad adopted all four children, bringing stability to the family. Finding his sweet grandmother collapsed on the floor, he watched emergency medical technicians rescue her and transport her to the hospital, kindling Bob's desire to be an EMT himself.

Throughout his early childhood and teen years, he was the target of bullies who discovered Bob's sensitive nature. Undiagnosed attention deficit disorder kept him on the edges of an educational system not yet prepared to handle his inattention, learning style, and behavior issues. Yet distractibility became Bob's best attribute, giving him a curious nature enabling him to explore a wide variety of interests.

In high school, Bob learned to play chess on his own. Instead of winning with the strength of the King or Queen, he learned to win with weakness. Chess taught Bob how to how to think and sometimes he won with lesser-ranked pawns or a knight. His father's friend affirmed him: "The strategies you use in this complex game, thinking eight to ten moves ahead and playing multiple games at the same time takes real intelligence. You are incredibly smart and don't let anyone tell you otherwise."

After graduating from high school in 1976, Bob still harbored a strong interest in medicine, but wasn't ready for college. He joined the U.S. Air Force and trained in x-ray technology and psychiatric evaluation. Bob screened service members with emotional difficulties, administered tests, and referred them to psychiatrists and the social services department when results indicated that need. As part of his training experiences, he took an IQ test and found out he wasn't as stupid as the kids in elementary school labeled him.

On March 27, 1977, a KLM 747 collided with a Pan Am 747 on the runway in Tenerife, the largest and most populous island of the Canary Islands. This tragic accident killed 583 people, the deadliest airline crash in history. The Air Force sent his more skilled work partner to the scene.

On return, his co-worker launched into grisly stories of mutilated corpses and human body parts littering the runway. In that pre-DNA era, dental records and wedding bands provided the only means of identification.

When Bob related a few of his buddy's stories to his Aunt Marie, a psychiatric nurse, she warned, "Don't get involved in that stuff. You are too young and inexperienced for that. It messes up your head." Years later, Bob reflected. *Wow, she was right about that.* Her prophetic words of wisdom stuck with him a long time.

While serving in the military in California, Bob worked with a young woman named Dixie, a born-again Christian. She and her husband, Roy, drove him nuts with their Gospel-and-Jesus-and-being-a-sinner talk. Despite their intense religious fervor, they became good friends. Dixie invited Bob to a spiritual retreat.

Bob's response? "Sorry. Not interested."

But for weeks, Dixie badgered him "You don't want to miss this. This retreat will change your life."

Trapped by Dixie and Roy into attending, a fuming Bob marched up to the retreat speaker and challenged him, "I'm a decent person. I try to live a good life. So I make a few mistakes. Why do I need to change my life?"

With two thick Bibles in hand, the speaker said, "Let's talk."

Using Bible verses, this godly man answered Bob's hostile questions, fired one after another. The more the retreat speaker shared, the more disarmed Bob felt. The speaker's warmth and genuine personality touched Bob's heart, and he began asking serious questions. The speaker spent all night pointing out Bible verse after Bible verse in response to Bob's challenges. He didn't mock Bob's questions or tire of his endless curiosities. His knowledge of the Bible impressed Bob.

Bob was no saint and carried a load of guilt. As he listened to this man share the Gospel, Bob's tone changed from being an obnoxious jerk to enjoying the question and answer dialog. That night Bob became a Christian and never turned back. This spiritual encounter in his twenties led him to believe God was in control of his life, and God had plans for Bob, just as promised in Jeremiah 29:11-14. *"For I know the plans that I have for you,' declares the Lord, 'plans for welfare and not for calamity to give you a future and a hope. Then you will call upon Me and come and pray to Me, and I will listen to you. You will seek Me and find Me when you search for Me with all your heart. I will be found by you,' declares the Lord . . .'"*

After the military, Bob was torn. His life interest in medicine pulled him one way, but his newfound faith also tugged at him. He enrolled in classes at Moody Bible Institute in Chicago, earned a Bachelor of Science in Christian Ministry, and met his wife, Sue. On May 29, 1982, Bob and Sue married, and ever since that day, he's affectionately called her Swaggy, a play on her maiden name. They've experienced their joys and trials, but they've clung together. Now married for 34 years, he's still devoted to her. Sue has been his rock, his best friend *ever*.

Throughout his adult life, Bob's been an eager learner. He wanted to know everything and do everything tied to emergency services and helping people in distress. As soon as he mastered one area of service, he stretched out to obtain training in a related area. He earned his National Registry of Emergency Medical Technicians Certificate, the higher-level EMT certificate, from Good Samaritan Hospital in Downers Grove, IL. He became a certified firefighter and worked for the Chicago Fire Department. Along the way he got his pilot's license; trained in post-traumatic stress disorders and critical incident stress management; earned an Associate in Applied Science Degree in Mortuary Science/Pathology with honors at Chicago Citywide College; completed his embalming internship at Cook County Morgue, Chicago, IL. and his pathology internship at Loyola Hospital, Maywood, IL.; received his Master Scuba Diver Certificate and served as an air-sea rescue scuba diver with the Chicago Fire Department; and earned a Masters in Pastoral Ministry and a Doctorate in Pastoral Ministry both at Christian Bible College and Seminary.

In their marriage, Bob and Sue suffered through health issues and heartache, yet their faith triumphed over fear. Sue suffered one miscarriage. She gave birth to a daughter, Heather, who was born hydrocephalic and endured twenty-five major surgeries, including brain surgery and open-heart surgery. They loved their child with special needs. Now independent, Heather lives in an apartment, earned an associate's degree in journalism, and works hard for a living. After launching their beloved three daughters into adulthood, Sue was diagnosed with breast cancer and underwent a mastectomy and chemo treatments.

Bob's personal understanding of suffering deepened his faith and commitment to compassionate care ministry. Volunteering as a chaplain at Ground Zero ripped Bob out of a comfortable world of calmness and routine into a world of chaos, despair, and suffering. This experience was the most significant work he ever faced in his life.

His background and experience in emergency services prepared him for Ground Zero, but not for the video loops of disturbing scenes playing through his mind long afterwards. Even as Chaplain Ossler offered comfort and hope to others, Bob struggled with significant emotional turmoil. The gruesome sights of recovered broken, mangled bodies buried amidst a fiery trash heap permeated his soul and challenged his mental equilibrium. Now, by the grace of God, he's moved through those horrible visions.

Fifteen years after 9/11, Bob Ossler serves as the Pastor of Visitation and Evangelism at Cumberland County Community Church in Millville, New Jersey. He also volunteers as a chaplain with the Millville, New Jersey Police Department. Once again, Chaplain Ossler works with severely traumatized people in the worst moments of their lives. Bob invites them to share their stressors and crisis as he shares the comfort of prayer and God's grace.

Janice Hall Heck, freelance writer and editor, retired from educational administration at Hong Kong International School in 2000. Heck then earned a master's degree in Biblical Counseling from Westminster Theological Seminary and worked as managing editor for the *Journal of Biblical Counseling.* She holds master's degrees in Special Education from Boston University and Public Administration/Educational Administration from College of Notre Dame, Belmont, CA.

Janice's entire teaching career involved working with children with learning and behavior problems. She taught special education classes in Franklin Township, NJ and in Beverly, MA. She moved to California and taught in a juvenile court school setting with adjudicated adolescents. After moving into educational administration, she worked as principal at North Star Elementary in Nikiski, AK, then later she became early childhood principal at Hong Kong International School.

After retiring, she taught English, writing, and computer applications at the New Jersey Recovery Services for adolescents with drug and alcohol addictions. She also directed those students in producing *News and Notes,* a student newsletter.

While in education, Heck presented workshops on teaching writing to children with special needs at school district and national conventions of the Council for Exceptional Children and the Association for Children with Learning Disabilities.

Heck authored *Evaluating and Improving Written Expression: A Practical Guide for Educators*, Allyn and Bacon, 1974; PRO-ED, 1986, 1999. She's been involved in writing critique groups for the 16 years. She's presented writing workshops at the Greater Philadelphia Christian Writers Conference. She was a member of the New Jersey Society of Christian Writers and now co-leads the Cumberland County Community Church Christian Writers' Critique Group. She's currently editor and publisher of *On the Horizon*, a quarterly 55+ community newsletter for Woods Landing, Mays Landing, NJ.

Photo Credits

Ground Zero Map on page 15: Derived from File: 911 -FEMA-Areas debris impact. Graphic.png by Therese McAllister, Jonathan Barnett, John Gross, Ronald Hamburger, Jon Magnuson of the Federal Emergency Management Agency (FEMA) of the United States Department of Homeland Security. As a work of the United States government, it was released to the public domain. It can be located on page 6 of the FEMA pdf located at http://www.fema.gov/pdf/library/fema403_ch1.pdf-study. Accessed June 15, 2016.

Please Note: The map was altered to show the location of St. Paul's Chapel. The floors hit by the two planes were also altered to match the facts listed in the 9/11 Museum's FAQ. Accessed June 15, 2016.

The photos on the pages listed below were used by permission.

Eble, Mary Gepana: pp. viii, 22, 24, 26, 37, 56, 58, 134, 139, 166

Domeij, Scoti: pp. vi, 1,60, 161, 174

Pennino, Dan: pp. 7, 9, 12, 44, 78, 79, 83

Schafer, Dan: pp. vi, iv, 1, 5, 17, 22, 34, 36, 37, 38, 46, 48, 49, 50, 52, 71, 75, 84, 86, 88, 95, 109, 119, 121, 124, 127, 133, 134, 152, 155, 158, 160, 161, 163

Photos provided by Lesley Visser, 145, 146

Prescott Valley Healing Field of Northern Arizona, p. 173

Appendix A: Chaplain's Toolbox: Spiritual Resources

"The Bible is filled with exciting and intense stories of love, war, birth, death and miracles. There's poetry, culture, history and theology. It's a suspense novel, a book of sociology, a history lesson—all woven around one eternal conflict: good versus evil."

—Max Lucado

Bob Ossler's toolbox held three major resources for his ministry: his Bible, prayer, and the "ABCDE of Faith." Caring for the immediate physical and emotional needs of others in crises is a primary goal in compassionate care ministry. The Bible, the source of healing power, opens the window of hope to eternity. Memorized Bible verses offer comfort when repeated in times of crisis. Bible stories offer broader answers, revealing how God helps sufferers work through distress. Prayer sparks our conversation and relationship with God, and the "ABCDE of Faith" offers a simple way to share our faith with others.

This appendix examines Ossler's three major tools, then provides four messages on suffering, troubles, and hope as seen in the lives of four biblical characters:

Joseph, a young man betrayed by his brothers, who offers forgiveness

Job, a wealthy, godly man, who loses everything

David, a shepherd boy who becomes a king, struggles through major conflicts in life

James, a follower of Jesus and a leader in the Jerusalem church, who warns of troubles in life.

Yes, we will experience heartache and hardship in this life, but in our suffering, we can reach out to God for comfort. With His help, we can triumph over adversity.

My Bible: Comfort, Guidance, and Window to Eternity

"Every hardship; every joy; every temptation is a challenge of the spirit; that the human soul may prove itself. The great chain of necessity wherewith we are bound has divine significance; and nothing happens which has not some service in working out the sublime destiny of the human soul."—Elias A. Ford

The Bible is a rich source for comfort and encouragement for those who suffer, offering guidelines for living and hope for the future. Without a doubt, it's an invaluable counseling manual and the most used implement in Bob's Chaplain's Toolbox.

My Bible: Comfort in Suffering

"Faith is believing an unshakable God when everything in me trembles and quakes."—Beth Moore

During my soul-searching moments at Ground Zero, I reread about how Jesus suffered in the Gospels. He was betrayed, rejected, arrested, falsely accused, mocked, wounded, scourged, cursed, humiliated, spat on, crucified, and left for dead. How much he endured.

My problems paled in comparison to Jesus' great sacrifice. The biggest complaints I mustered on the Pile? "Momentary, light afflictions" (2 Corinthians 4:17); irritating gravel in my boots; damp, cold weather; gritty food and drink; obnoxious smells . . . all bearable things. The presence of death all around me induced depression and anxiety, but these feelings also were not greater than the crucifixion of Jesus.

Jesus' story didn't end with His agonizing death. After three days, He arose from the dead. He later ascended into heaven to be with His Father, and our Father, where Jesus promised to prepare a place for us: *"Do not let your heart be troubled; believe in God, believe also in Me. In My Father's house are many dwelling places; if it were not so, I would have told you; for I go to prepare a place for you. If I go and prepare a place for you, I will come again and receive you to Myself, that where I am, there you may be also."* (John 14:1-3)

Reading my Bible restored my emotional balance, bringing me back to a more spiritual place so I could listen to and counsel others who struggled with their emotions. I found so much help in the Word of God. Anytime I gave a mini-sermon after a recovery at Ground Zero or shared caring words with families, I'd open my Bible to a relevant portion of Scripture and share how these verses helped me personally.

When people needed compassionate spiritual care, I turned to Psalm 23, a psalm familiar to many: *"The LORD is my shepherd. I shall not want. He makes me lie down in green pastures; He leads me beside quiet waters. He restores my soul; He guides me in the paths of righteousness."* Under any circumstances, we can trust Him to steer us the right way.

Many other beautiful psalms also consoled myself and others: *"He who dwells in the shelter of the Most High will abide in the shadow of the Almighty. I will say to the LORD, 'MY REFUGE AND MY FORTRESS, MY GOD, IN WHOM I TRUST!'"* (PSALM 91:1-2) To sufferers in serious need of emotional and spiritual support, these verses offer a poetic, yet clear, invitation to a troubled heart to rest.

And what is the outcome of receiving comfort from our God in the Scriptures? We recognize pain and suffering in others. Our hearts connect with their hearts, and we offer the same comfort we received from God and Scripture, just as Paul, the apostle of Jesus Christ, described in 2 Corinthians 1:3-5: *"Blessed be the God and Father of our Lord Jesus Christ, the Father of mercies and God of all comfort, Who comforts us in all our affliction so that we will be able to comfort those who are in any affliction with the comfort with which we ourselves are comforted by God. For just as the sufferings of Christ are ours in abundance, so also our comfort is abundant through Christ.*

The Bible doesn't promise us a perfect life or one without pain and suffering. In fact, James 1:2-4 warns of difficult times, of trials and tribulations. But remember this: in the vast expanse of time and infinity, our lives on earth are only as a split second; our troubles only momentary, light afflictions; but our healing and future with God lasts for eternity.

Though we have trouble now, we will receive peace and healing later. This is our comfort in our sorrow. And this comfort we can share with others.

My Bible: Guidance for Everyday Living

"The Bible was not given for our information but for our transformation."—D.L. Moody

No issue or problem in life is so big that the Bible doesn't provide commentary. Of course, I come from a Christian perspective and many might argue the Bible is all "God stuff" and "religion," and they don't want to be "preached at."

I once maintained those attitudes myself, until one day I discovered the richness and beauty of the Bible. The best counseling tool ever written, my Bible became my soothing poetry, my wisdom, my wake-up call, and my To-Do list for life.

As a Bible student, I learned to value and follow 2 Timothy 3:16-17: *"All Scripture is inspired by God and profitable for teaching, for reproof, for correction, for training in righteousness; so that the man of God may be adequate, equipped for every good work."*

Hebrews 4:12 comments on how the Bible judges *"the thoughts and intentions of the heart."* Romans 15:4 offers hope and encouragement for living a life that honors God.

When people asked at Ground Zero how they should live, I shared the practical everyday advice in Galatians 5:22-26: *"But the fruit of the Spirit is love, joy, peace, patience, kindness, goodness, faithfulness, gentleness, self-control; against such things there is no law. Now those who belong to Christ Jesus have crucified the flesh with its passions and desires. If we live by the Spirit, let us also walk by the Spirit. Let us not become boastful, challenging one another, envying one another."*

Can you imagine? If individuals, communities, states, and nations lived by these qualities, how different would life and our world be? Develop these qualities in your life, and you will do well.

A whole host of Scripture passages advise seekers on how to live godly lives: *"Finally , brethren, whatever is true, whatever is honorable, whatever is right, whatever is pure, whatever is lovely, whatever is of good repute, if there is any excellence and if anything worthy of praise, dwell on these things. The things you have learned and received and heard and seen in me, practice these things, and the God of peace will be with you."* (Philippians 4:8-9)

Your actions reflect your beliefs and speak louder than words. *"Don't copy the behavior and customs of this world, but let God transform you into a new person by changing the way you think. Then you will learn to know God's will for you, which is good and pleasing and perfect."* Romans 12:1-2 (NLT), *". . . you are a letter of Christ, cared for by us, written not with ink but with the Spirit of the living God, not on tablets of stone but on tablets of human hearts."* (2 Corinthians 3:3)

You can discover this treasure trove of guidance for yourself. As President Ronald Reagan observed, "Within the covers of the Bible are the answers for all problems men face."

My Bible: Hope for Eternity

> *"This book [the Bible] tells the grandest, most compelling story of all time: the story of a true God who loves His children, who established for them a way of salvation and provided a route to eternity."*—Max Lucado

More than anything else, the Bible gives us promises for the future and offers a path to salvation which leads to eternal life with God, just as John 3:16 promises. *"For God so loved the world, that He gave His only begotten Son, that whoever believes in Him shall not perish, but have eternal life."*

Scripture reassures us that we don't need to fear death or grieve as those who have no hope (I Thessalonians 4:13). The hope of healing and living with God in eternity gives us the courage to grieve through suffering and tragic losses. Our hope and comfort assures us of being reunited with loved ones in eternity.

The Bible promises a time when sorrow, tears, pain, and death will no longer hold dominion over us. *"And I heard a loud voice from the throne, saying, 'Behold, the tabernacle of God is among men, and He will dwell among them, and they shall be His people, and God Himself will be among them, and He will wipe away every tear from their eyes; and there will no longer be any death; there will*

no longer be any mourning, or crying, or pain; the first things have passed away.'"
(Revelation 21:3-4)

Life Lessons about Suffering, Troubles, and Hope

"The Bible is the greatest of all books; to study it is the noblest of all pursuits; to understand it. The highest of all goals."—Charles C. Ryrie

We don't know how our lives will turn out, or where the twists and turns, starts and stops, hiccoughs and coughs will take us. Some life crises seem so devastating that we think we will never move through them: terrorist attacks; death of a spouse, child, family member or close friend; major debilitating or chronic illness; betrayal and divorce; financial disaster or bankruptcy; or natural disasters.

You think, *Where is God? Why has God forgotten me? Why do I have to carry such pain? Why can't my family and friends understand how I'm suffering? Why? Why? Why?*

These questions are the same questions many Bible characters posed. Anything that happens to us has already happened to someone in the Bible and to someone near you. However, that does not minimize our pain. My pain, your pain is real and long-lasting. Even those with deep faith experience devastating emotional pain. The Bible reminds us that we're not alone, and we can find peace, if only for moments at a time, in God's Word and with God's people.

Reciting memorized Bible verses in moments of stress can calm your spirit. Singing a verse or two of your favorite hymn may do the same. Praying or talking with a small group of trusted friends provides encouragement. Reading stories of pain and suffering in the Bible soothes grief and suffering. The stories of godly men and women who went through these trials and tribulations offer hope for healing, if not for now, in our future.

Joseph: Betrayed by Family

"Forgiveness is the fragrance the violet sheds on the heel that has crushed it."—Mark Twain

Consider Joseph in the book of Genesis. Acting out of jealous motives, his brothers sold Joseph, their father's favorite son, to a band of traders heading to Egypt. Removing their despised brother's annoying presence from their lives inflicted excruciating pain on their beloved father, Jacob, who grieved the loss of his son by tearing his clothes and putting on the sackcloth of mourning. Refusing to be comforted, he wept bitterly.

Years later, due to a famine in their land, the starving, deceitful brothers begged for food from Joseph, now a high official in Egypt. After a short time of testing, Joseph forgave his brothers and said: *"As for you, you meant evil against me, but God meant it for good in order to bring about this present result, to preserve many people alive."* (Genesis 50:20)

Indeed, Joseph's faith in God and his foresight and planning to avoid the effects of a multi-country famine saved the Egyptian population from starvation. And he was reunited with his father and brothers.

Many biblical stories fit this pattern: an incident or crisis initially perceived as harmful returns as a blessing years later. Crises trigger greater spiritual awakening. Theologian Tim Keller says this, *"I learned that just as many people find God through affliction and suffering. They find that adversity moves them toward God rather than away. Troubled times awaken them out of their haunted sleep of spiritual self-sufficiency into a serious search for the divine."*

Four hundred years later, after generations of God's blessing and prosperity for Joseph's family in Egypt, the Hebrew immigrants grew in strength to over two million. The Egyptians began to fear them. A new pharaoh enslaved them, forcing them to perform hard labor, and then ordered the Hebrew midwives to kill newborn baby boys.

A young Hebrew mother feared the Egyptians would kill her three-month-old baby so she tucked him into a basket of reeds and hid him in the bulrushes by the river. Pharaoh's daughter saw the baby, recognized that it was a Hebrew baby, and felt sorry for him.

Through a godly chain of events, Pharaoh's daughter hired the mother of the baby to care for the infant. Pharaoh's daughter saved this child's life. She saved a mother from major grief, and ultimately, she saved a person who became a great leader of the Hebrew nation.

His name? Moses, a man who, after crises of his own, led the Hebrews from their suffering out of Egypt to the Promised Land. However, their hardships did not end immediately. The Hebrews wandered for forty years in the Sinai desert before arriving in the Promised Land. During their long journey, God provided daily manna from heaven and water from a rock.

Job: Devastated by Loss

"God whispers to us in our pleasures, speaks in our conscience, but shouts in our pain: it is His megaphone to rouse a deaf world."—C. S. Lewis, *The Problem of Pain*

A blameless and upright man, Job feared God and shunned evil. Job received messages carried from afar by four different servants. Two servants told of attacks by neighboring invaders, the Sabeans and the Chaldeans, who raided two of his camps and carried off his entire holdings there: 500 yoke of oxen, 500 donkeys, 3000 camels, and servants. Two more messengers arrived and relayed news of natural disasters. A fire from the sky burned up his 7000 sheep along with their attending servants. Then a great wind collapsed his house killing his seven sons and three daughters who were all inside together having a family celebration. But that's not all. In his mourning, Job contracted painful sores over every inch of his body.

In his abundance, Job easily worshipped and praised God. After losing his family and livelihood, how would he worship and praise God in his grief? Despite the sarcasm and taunting of his wife to "Curse God and die!", Job kept his faith and did not blame God.

Job's friends visited Job in his ashes and sackcloth of mourning. They wept, tore their garments, sprinkled dust on their heads, and joined Job in his sorrow. "*Then they sat down on the ground with him for seven days and seven nights with no one speaking a word to him, for they saw that his pain was very great."* (Job 2:13)

It is not unusual for a person in deep grieving to question God's purposes, and Job was not immune to these doubts. Self-pity came to his lips. His friends challenged him to speak against God. In the end, after a lengthy discourse, God spoke to Job firmly and reminded him of who was in charge of the earth. *"Then the LORD answered Job out of the whirlwind and said, 'Where were you when I laid the foundation of the earth? Tell Me, if you have understanding, Who set its measurements? Since you know. Or who stretched the line on it? On what were its bases sunk? Or who laid its cornerstone, when the morning stars sang together and all the sons of God shouted for joy?'"* (Job 38:1, 4-7)

God asked Job many more questions, stunning him into submission. Job finally realized his place in God's plan. *"Then Job answered the LORD AND SAID, 'I KNOW THAT YOU CAN DO ALL THINGS, AND THAT NO PURPOSE OF YOURS CAN BE THWARTED . . . THEREFORE I HAVE DECLARED THAT WHICH I DID NOT UNDERSTAND, THINGS TOO WONDERFUL FOR ME, WHICH I DID NOT KNOW.'"* (JOB 42:1-3)

Job processed the emotions in dealing with his losses: self-pity, doubt, questioning God's purposes, and finally acceptance and healing. Even though Job challenged God, He never abandoned Job.

When bad things happen to people, how do we respond? Do we blame God? Do we lose our faith or do we grow in our faith? The answers to these questions determine whether we'll triumph over suffering.

David: Troubled by Conflict

"What I see in the Bible, especially in the book of Psalms, which is a book of gratitude for the created world, is a recognition that all good things on Earth are God's, every good gift is from above."—Philip Yancey

The beautiful, powerful passage of Psalm 23 can be used in inspirational messages and for meditation at any time. David, a shepherd in his early life and later the king of the great nation, Israel, wrote Psalm 23 from his experiences of escaping life-threatening crises to finding security in the arms of God. Put yourself in this psalm to find the peace you seek.

Psalm 23:1: The Good Shepherd

"The LORD is my shepherd I shall not be in want."—Psalm 23:1

Sheep depend on the shepherd for everything: a sheltered spot in which to rest, green pastures, clean water to drink and protection from harm. The sheep trust him with their lives. They know his voice and follow him wherever he leads. The Lord is our Good Shepherd. He provides for us and comforts us in our sorrows when we follow and trust Him.

But you ask, "What about the terrorist attacks that just happened and the pain and sorrow generated by this evil act? What about the loss of so many people? And what about other problems in our lives that bring pain? What about deaths of loved ones? What about serious illnesses or diseases in my family? What about accidents and injuries that change our lives? What about the pain and sorrow and anger we feel? How can God comfort us when we're distraught and hopeless? How can we be comforted when we are beyond comfort?

God never promised freedom from pain in this world. In fact, the Bible tells us the opposite. *"These things I have spoken to you, so that in Me you may have peace. In the world you will have tribulation, but take courage; I have overcome the world."* (John 16:33)

God offers help and comfort in the Bible. He has not forgotten you. You are special to Him.

He created you. *"I will give thanks to You, for I am fearfully and wonderfully made; wonderful are Your works, and my soul knows it very well."* (Psalm 139:13-14)

He knows you. *"I am the good shepherd, and I know My own and My own know Me, even as the Father knows Me and I know the Father; and I lay down My life for the sheep. I have other sheep, which are not of this fold; I must bring them also, and they will hear My voice; and they will become one flock with one shepherd."* (John 10:14-16)

He engraved your name on His hand. *"Behold, I have inscribed you on the palms of My hands . . ."* (Isaiah 49:16)

He counts your tears. *"You have taken account of my wanderings; put my tears in Your bottle. Are they not in Your book?"* (Psalm 56:8)

Our Good Shepherd loves us. He wants us to depend on Him for our needs and concerns. Go to God and give your burdens and pain to Him. Rest in faith and prayer.

Psalm 23:2: Green Pastures

"He makes me lie down in green pastures; He leads me beside quiet waters."—Psalm 23:2

Picture this setting of peace prepared for us by God. A flock of content, woolly sheep resting in a lush green pasture, their shepherd standing by guarding against the threat of starving wild animals. The sheep listen for the shepherd's commands and obediently respond to his voice and his leading. They trust their guardian with their lives.

Smell the scents of colorful flowers and fresh mowed grass. Feel the warmth of the sun and the warm breezes against your skin. See the butterflies flutter through air. Hear the birds tweeting sweet songs and a meandering brook rippling over a rocky streambed. Feel refreshed by the sights and sounds of God's handiwork.

Envision this tranquil place where worries and cares disappear. Your guardian Shepherd keeps watch nearby. If you stray from the path and get lost, He searches for you. If you fall, He picks you up. If you're sad, He comforts you. Relax in these green pastures and think of God and His Son, Jesus.

Psalm 23:3: Paths of Righteousness

"He restores my soul; He guides me in the paths of righteousness for His name's sake."—Psalm 23:3

The Lord asks us to rest and relax while He handles our burdens for us. He's in charge. He wants us to lay our concerns in His lap. He restores our souls and refreshes us for the next bout with life, just as Matthew 11:28-29 expresses: *"Come to Me, all who are weary and heavy-laden, and I will give you rest. Take My yoke upon you and learn from Me, for I am gentle and humble in heart, and YOU WILL FIND REST FOR YOUR SOULS."*

Psalm 23:4: Valley of Shadow of Death

"Even though I walk through the valley of the shadow of death, I fear no evil for You are with me, Your rod and Your staff they comfort me."—Psalm 23:4

God never promised we'd live life free from pain in this world. In fact, James 1:2-4 tells us the opposite: *"Consider it all joy, my brethren, when you encounter various trials knowing that the testing of your faith produces endurance. And let endurance have its perfect result, so that you may be perfect and complete, lacking in nothing."*

Death, darkness, and destruction surrounded us on the Pile. In the dark, depressing valley of the shadow of death we see no light, and we lose hope. The world is a tough, mean place at times. Evil exists. We don't need to fear evil: God will help us through hard times. And in turn, we help others as they struggle.

Troubles can come from terrorists wreaking havoc or they can hit closer to home: death of a family member or close friend, loss of a job and financial security, chronic pain or terminal illness, separation or divorce in a family, verbal, physical, or sexual abuse. Buried in the valley of the shadow of death, what could be worse? How will we survive? Terrible thoughts fill our minds and hearts, and we see no escape.

Even when we know and trust God, we'll still encounter fears, dangers, and hardships. However, when horrible calamities happen, we can turn to Him and share our anxieties and concerns.

Though time spent in the dark valley is hard, many times we come through the trouble with a clearer vision of how God works in our lives. In good times, we think we're self-sufficient, and we ignore God. But in hard times, when we know we cannot go on alone, we turn to God. God desires for us to be faithful to Him all the time, through good times and hard times. With God walking alongside us through the valley of the shadow of death, we can emerge triumphant.

Recalling struggles in our dark valleys and how God stayed close encourages us when facing new valleys. Struggling through pain-filled days helps us comfort others in their times of trouble. (2 Corinthians 1:3-5)

Psalm 23:5: My Cup of Blessings

"You prepare a table before me in the presence of my enemies; You have anointed my head with oil; My cup overflows." —Psalm 23:5

When we emerge from the deep, dark valley, it's time to celebrate. God prepares a great table of abundance and grace for us even though enemies and darkness still surround us. We sit safely inside His kingdom. Our enemies lie beyond the high walls of the king's compound.

In biblical times, a host honored his guests with expensive ointments. The fragrant oil moisturized the skin and promoted healing and overall good feeling. Our cup overflows the abundant blessings God provides, and we can be thankful for safety in God's presence.

Psalm 23:6: The House of the Lord

"Surely goodness and lovingkindness will follow me all the days of my life, and I will dwell in the house of the Lord FOREVER."—Psalm 23:6

Here is our glimpse of eternity. Here is the promise and our hope as we struggle through our earthly troubles: We will live in perfect peace with God forever in eternity. *"Behold, the tabernacle of God is among men, and He will dwell among them, and they shall be His people, and God Himself will be among them, and He will wipe away every tear from their eyes; and there will no longer be any death; there will no longer be any mourning, or crying, or pain; the first things have passed away."* (Revelation 21:3-4)

Being in the House of the Lord is beyond our comprehension. We can only imagine the greatness and glory of its structure, but our imaginings will only be an inkling of the true beauty of His house. He promises joy in His presence, along with peace and safety and freedom from worry and sorrows. There in the safety of His House, we can seek to grow in our spiritual relationship with Him, we can honor Him, and we can follow in His footsteps.

This is His message to us: *"For I know the plans that I have for you,' declares the LORD, 'plans for welfare and not for calamity to give you a future and a hope. Then you will call upon Me and come and pray to Me, and I will listen to you. You will seek Me and find Me when you search for Me with all your heart. I will be found by you,' declares the Lord."* (Jeremiah 29:11-14) God wants to meet us in our suffering and He wants to seek Him out in our suffering.

James: Joy in Trials and Difficult Times

> *"Wisdom is not primarily knowing the truth, although it certainly includes that; it is skill in living. For, what good is a truth if we don't know how to live it? What good is an intention if we can't sustain it?"*—Eugene H. Peterson.

James, the brother of Jesus and a leader in the Jerusalem church, wrote a letter the Epistle of James to Christians. Escaping from Israel because of persecution, Christians settled in Rome, Alexandria, and other cities in Greece and Asia Minor and around the Mediterranean Sea. Despite their troubles, he encouraged them to stand firm in their new locations and cultures. James's message about handling life's trials resonates for us in current times.

Going in and out of St. Paul's chapel, I noticed priests or chaplains conducting spiritual services. Many Ground Zero workers and volunteers relaxed and listened through the meditations, prayers, and encouraging talks. These healing services prompted a measure of peace and consolation to exhausted workers.

I took a turn giving a talk and focused on James 1: 2-8. *"Consider it all joy, my brethren, when you encounter various trials, knowing that the testing of your faith produces endurance. And let endurance have its perfect result, so that you may be perfect and complete, lacking in nothing. But if any of you lacks wisdom, let him ask of God, who gives to all generously and without reproach, and it will be given to him. But he must ask in faith without any doubting, for the one who doubts is like the surf of the sea, driven and tossed by the wind. For that man ought not to expect that he will receive anything from the Lord, being a double-minded man, unstable in all his ways."*

James 1:2: Life's Trials and Joy

"Consider it all joy, my brethren when you encounter various trials . . ."—James 1:2

Pure joy?

Who would ever find pure joy in a trial? In a terrorist attack? In human death and suffering?

After experiencing the most horrible terror attacks on American soil, you say, "Have pure joy?" Absolute destruction surrounds us, and we hurt so badly inside. In the midst of carnage and death with no immediate relief in sight, we're frazzled and fatigued beyond what we normally handle. We're experiencing a catastrophe that none of us could have ever imagined in our lives.

Joy? How can we find joy in this tragedy? Perhaps we need to change the question.

Will we ever move through the agony and mourning to a better place? Maybe not.

Our memories store these events and our pain for a long time. Our hearts will ache and our tears will flow each time a memory trigger launches us back to those devastating scenes that inflicted so much pain. Each anniversary of the event, each reminder, will stir up our loss, sadness and heartache.

Can we grow stronger from this? Probably.

Trials build character and strength. Confidence in triumphing over a tragedy, no matter how horrible or awful, allows us to proclaim we overcame the crisis with God's help.

In times of shared tragedy, everyone around us pulls together. The event of 9/11 is just one example. We organized to restore order to our lives, our city, our country. I felt fortified in all the work we accomplished.

Biblical joy, which means a change in our perspective, infuses us with hope and assurance that we can overcome and grow through a horrible event and unsettled times.

We come to understand that as we call on the Lord, we can regain our mental, emotional, physical, and spiritual strength. Over time, we'll regain a positive gait in our walk, a spring in our step, a smile on our face, a joy in our hearts.

We all encounter our various personal trials and tribulation at one time or another. Now as I look back at some of my most difficult trials, the enormity of the struggle humbles me. I recognize how God walked alongside me through each challenge.

We all can tell our stories of adversities. Suffering exempts no one. Over the years, I've prayed with hundreds of hurting people. At the time I prayed with them, their pain seemed immeasurable. Now they're beyond their trial and doing better. However, they've not forgotten their loved ones or their terrible problem. Because *"The Lord is near to the brokenhearted and saves those who are crushed in spirit"* (Psalm 34:18), we can trust God to move with us through the mourning journey.

James 1:3: Life's Trials Test our Faith

". . . the testing of your faith produces endurance."—James 1:3

You've got to be kidding me. A crisis will increase my endurance?

Oh, yes, the terrorist attack tested our faith, however, the perpetrators failed to understand the resilience of Americans, and how we pick ourselves up and turn to God. We endured attacks on our homeland, and we grew stronger even as we struggled on the battle lines of Ground Zero. With God's help, our strength, energy, and fighting attitude overcame all odds.

The testing of our faith produces endurance. After this horrible attack, I witnessed people's faith grow by leaps and bounds. A lot of folks turned to God in so many ways. Religious services filled up. Prayer circles and lines formed in so many places on the Pile and around the perimeter. Many voiced high expectations: "We shall overcome." Others turned to God or renewed their relationships with God. The attacks on the World Trade Center inspired a spiritual revival for many people.

We also witnessed a different type of victory: Volunteering abounded. Love of fellow man exploded. People hugged and cared for one another. Strangers extended kindnesses. Others lifted up fellow workers in prayer. People embraced their faith and experienced a beauty they never thought they'd see. Courage, strength, and dignity rose to a whole new level. People talked about God openly and prayed in public. What an amazing, heartwarming happening, to witness this change in attitudes. We persevered through the tragedy and devastation, and one amazing result was seeing spiritual growth in people's lives.

Where was all this community spirit and love of God before? Where neighbors hardly spoke to neighbors and strangers remained strangers? This tragedy drew out the best in people—almost like a revival on a grander scale. Love thy neighbor, serve thy neighbor, pray for thy neighbor. This tragedy definitely tested our faith, almost to the limits for some and possibly further for others. However, the testing of our faith produced endurance.

James 1:4: Life's Trials Produce Endurance

"...let endurance have its perfect result, so that you may be perfect and complete, lacking in nothing."—James 1:4

Endurance. What was James talking about in James 1:4? After the terrorist attack, we saw our world and our relationships in a much different light. Our attitudes and affections changed. We cared for our families, friends, and acquaintances unlike never before. We reached out to bring solace to others. Men and women, rich and poor, from all walks of life grew and learned to love one another.

No, it wasn't a big hug fest or kum-ba-ya at the campfire; it was stronger than that. People expressed genuine caring to those who suffered the loss of loved ones. Kindness abounded at a level I'd never seen before. Hundreds of people offered help; donated food, supplies, or money; took time off from work; used vacation time to volunteer; provided transportation; or did whatever needed to be done—all out of the compassion in their hearts.

Oh, I could not write in a single paragraph about all the acts of compassion I witnessed in New York City. I experienced a kinder, gentler, caring from others for their fellow man as never before. Yes, we grew by leaps and bounds in our love of our Lord and fellow man. A maturity surged from the wells of our hearts. No longer naïve about life, love and hope—faith in action—streamed from our newfound courage and endurance.

James 1:5-8: Wisdom, Prayer, and Faith

> *"But if any of you lacks wisdom, let him ask of God, who gives to all generously and without reproach, and it will be given to him. But he must ask in faith without any doubting, for the one who doubts is like the surf of the sea, driven and tossed by the wind. For that man ought not to expect that he will receive anything from the Lord, being a double-minded man, unstable in all his ways."—James 1:5-8*

You may be thinking, "I have nothing but doubts today. How can you be so sure that I can ask God for wisdom?"

I saw countless people turn to God in prayer and ask specific prayers. I prayed without ceasing and received answers. Of course, these were not prayers for material possessions for me, but they were prayers for the needs of others and for wisdom to handle these trying times.

People turned up their spiritual reliance on God a notch and were shocked and awed at how God provided. Swift answers to prayers for physical needs at Ground Zero shook people. I know in the past I prayed and secretly doubted answers would ever come. But that didn't happen at the Pile. No doubts there. Stories of many answered prayers abound. Prayers answered before I privately whispered them to God. I became aware of the answer only after I prayed.

We asked God for help, and He answered in mighty ways. Faith overcame doubt. Now we feel closer to God and trust Him in all we do. Yes, we grew from the tragic events of 9/11. We're still growing in our faith.

I pray that even more people will experience spiritual growth and trust our awesome God through good times and bad.

Prayer: A.C.T.S.: Adoration, Confession, Thanksgiving, Supplication

"Jesus never taught His disciples how to preach, only how to pray. He did not speak much of what was needed to preach well, but much of praying well. To know how to speak to God is more than knowing how to speak to man. Not power with men, but power with God is the first thing."—Andrew Murray

Ministry is hard work, but it's God's work. Family members or friends frequently ask me to visit hospitals, nursing homes, prisons, or private homes with the specific focus to pray or share the Gospel with their loved ones. Some ask me to visit because they're uncomfortable praying or talking about God in front of family members; others want a fresh voice speaking to their loved one about God. God has given me both a talkative nature and eagerness to pray in any situation, for anyone, at any time.

Pastoral visitation gives me the opportunity to share the truths of the Bible without preaching. I spent time with a man in a coma who almost died. With his family's permission, I prayed the Gospel in his ear. "Lord, I ask you to remove this dear man from the valley of the shadow of death. He doesn't need to fear evil because You are with him in this trial. You, God, know we're all sinners, yet You give us a chance to confess our sins. We all have sinned and fallen short of the glory of God."

We prayed earnestly for this loved one to recover, yet realizing he might not. I visited him in rehab on his slow road to recovery. We talked together about God and eternal life. I shared a few Bible verses with him and asked if he wanted to give his life to Jesus. He silently confessed to God, and then prayed to ask Jesus into his heart. His heart softened, and he grinned from ear to ear. Many people prayed privately for this man and his wife. His journey was still long, but brighter.

Prayer glorifies God and shows people the power He displays. I've seen critically ill people get better after prayer and ultimately recover. I've been with people who were about to be unplugged from life support come out of a coma and recover. People with hardened hearts come to know the Lord through prayer.

God sometimes answers our prayers in unexpected ways. Sometimes the answer we desire does not arrive. We don't always understand God's plan that's different from ours. In these cases, we acknowledge God's wisdom and power, knowing He's in charge.

Without prayer at Ground Zero, I'd have been a blubbering idiot. Even though I felt called to be there, being around people with such desperate emotional and spiritual needs proved grueling. Prayer, quiet devotion, and reflection about God's greatness and goodness cleared out heavy thoughts and memories and I regained inner peace and strength through God's power.

Nothing else, other than reading my Bible, brought me as much relief from the stress of ministering at Ground Zero as prayer.

Prayer: Conversation with God

"Prayer is not a privilege for the pious, not the art of a chosen few. Prayer is simply the heartfelt conversation between God and the child."—Max Lucado

Prayers can be long or short, aloud or silent, said or sung. There's no right or wrong way to pray. Our primary purpose is to honor God and not just beg for selfish desires. The sequence of ideas in prayer makes no difference. God just wants to hear sincere thoughts from our hearts.

When I prayed with people at Ground Zero, I used an informal format for my words: Adoration, Confession, Thanksgiving, and Supplication (A.C.T.S.). My prayers were short, simple, and clear so listeners caught the nugget of God's Word to carry with them throughout the day.

While a useful acronym and model for prayer, A.C.T.S. is, by no means, rigid or the only way to pray. The Lord's Prayer, the most recited prayer in Christian gatherings, includes elements of adoration, confession, thanksgiving, and supplication, although not in that order.

When you pray, remember these keywords, then elaborate on the ideas in your prayers.

Lord, Teach Us to Pray

"It happened that while Jesus was praying in a certain place, after He had finished, one of His disciples said to Him, 'Lord, teach us to pray . . .'"—(Luke 11:1)

Before Jesus's baptism and entry into ministry, He prayed. (Luke 3:21-22) After performing miracles and during crises, Jesus prayed. (Matthew 14:14-23; John 6:1-15; Luke 5:15-16; Matthew 26:1-36) Jesus's disciples witnessed Jesus pray for them and for others (John 1-12; Matthew 19:13; John 17:9, 20; Luke 9:28). His disciples were aware that Jesus rose early to pray (Mark 1:35), sometimes prayed all night (Luke 6:12), and withdrew to pray alone (Luke 22:4), as Psalm 46:10 counsels, *"Be still, and know that I am God."*

Jesus prayed when His heart was troubled and even cried while praying (John 12:27-28; Hebrews 5:7) In the last moments of His life with nails piercing his wrists and feet, Jesus prayed for others (Luke 23:34, 46)—and for his enemies (Luke 23:33-34).

Jesus chided hypocrites who "practice their righteousness" by standing and praying in the synagogues and on street corners to be seen by all. He pointed out that the customs of the prayer-ignorant, who did not worship the true God, just babbled meaningless repetitions, thinking their words were heard. (Matthew 6:5-7) For His disciples, Jesus prayed for strength (Luke 22:32) and for protection from the evil one. (John 17:1:15). During the hard times of my life and at Ground Zero, Jesus's example of seeking out His heavenly Father through prayer was my role model.

N. T. Wright wrote: "For the Lord's Prayer is not so much a command as an invitation: an invitation to share in the prayer-life of Jesus himself." When the disciples asked Jesus to teach them to pray, He invited His disciples to praise and pray in private to His Father and in this manner: *"Pray, then, in this way: 'Our Father who is in heaven, hallowed be Your name. Your kingdom come. Your will be done, On earth as it is in heaven. Give us this day our daily bread. And forgive us our debts, as we also have forgiven our debtors. And do not lead us into temptation, but deliver us from evil. [For Yours is the kingdom and the power and the glory forever. Amen.'"]* (Matthew 6:9-13)

A: Adoration for God

> *"Our Father who is in heaven, hallowed be Your name. Your kingdom come. Your will be done, on earth as it is in heaven."—Matthew 6:9-10*

The first verses of the Lord's Prayer focuses on honoring, revering, adoring, and worshipping Who God says He is. Being human, our earthy fathers may or may not have fulfilled all of our expectations, and may have on numerous occasions disappointed us. Each of us has an earthly father—good, bad or indifferent—and our earthly father influences our mental image of our heavenly Father

Our heavenly Father does not disappoint. Our Heavenly Father is a Father we can trust. As the head of our family and the Father of our brothers and sisters, He loves us, hears our prayers, and carries our burdens. God created us, and to show appreciation, we praise and honor Him. His kingdom is our workplace; our purpose is to serve Him in this kingdom. To do His will joyfully, we serve Him by serving others, not to earn rewards, but to show our love for God and desire to serve Him.

As you begin your prayer, offer praise to God. In both the Old and New Testaments, prayers begin by adoring God as does this prayer in Psalm 68:35: *"O God, You are awesome from Your sanctuary. The God of Israel Himself gives strength and power to the people. Blessed be God!"*

C: Confession to God

> *"And forgive us our debts, as we also have forgiven our debtors . . ."*
> *—Matthew 6:12*

Bitterness. Anger. Unforgiveness. Selfishness. Jealousy. Greed. Lust. Overindulgence. Envy. Pride. Apathy. Lying. . .who hasn't experienced these temptations?

The Lord's Prayer touches on our actions and attitudes in one word: debts. But God desires we be specific in private prayer. Everyone regrets inappropriate choices. We know what those choices are. God knows what they are, too, but He wants to hear us put them into words. When we put our misdeeds into words, we acknowledge our wrongdoing and show our heartfelt sorrow.

Debts require payment.

Transgressions require justice.

Sinful behaviors require forgiveness.

When we acknowledge our sins, we remember that through God's grace and compassion, His Son, Jesus Christ paid the debt for our sins. He hears our confessions, offering forgiveness just as 1 John 1:9 tells us: *"If we confess our sins, He is faithful and righteous to forgive us our sins and to cleanse us from all unrighteousness."*

As we become more Christ-like, our ways of relating to the world change, even though the world's temptations stay within reach. In our prayers, we constantly ask God to help us avoid things which tempt us and detract from our relationship with God.

T: Thanksgiving for Our Blessings

"I will praise the name of God with song and magnify Him with thanksgiving."—Psalm 69:30

When we honor God, we acknowledge His greatness and all-powerful-ness. With thanksgiving, we go before God, gratefully naming what He's given us and done for us. Even though some things did not seem good at the time, these negative events often led to blessings.

Many people who suffered great sorrows later acknowledged these same troubles brought them closer to God, and difficult experiences changed their lives in positive ways. We do not forget our troubles or losses, but with God's help, we put them in perspective.

We all welcome appreciation or thank-you notes when we do something thoughtful for someone. In like manner, thank God for the many blessings He provides on a daily basis. In 1897, Johnson Oatman published a hymn familiar to many today. *Count Your Blessings* (copyright, public domain).

> *When upon life's billows you are tempest-tossed,*
> *When you are discouraged, thinking all is lost,*
> *Count your many blessings, name them one by one,*
> *And it will surprise you what the Lord has done.*

S: Supplication: Earnest Appeals to God

"Give us this day our daily bread . . . And do not lead us into temptation, but deliver us from evil."—Matthew 6:11; 13

Asking God for basic needs everyday shows trust and dependence on Him. But notice the words "our daily bread." Our. Daily. Bread.

Our. God asks us to pray for *our* brother and sisters as well as for ourselves. In turn, God uses others to help answer their prayers and yours. *"The King will answer and say to them, 'Truly I say to you, to the extent that you did it to one of these brothers of Mine, even the least of them, you did it to Me.'"* (Matthew 25:40)

Daily. Everyday. Without fail. This day. This week. This year. In all the days ahead in the future.

Bread. The basic necessities of life: food, shelter, clothing, relationships. Remember one more thing: spiritual bread. Yearning to be more Christ-like in daily living is part of our prayers.

Humbly and earnestly, make your appeals to God. Ask for specific needs in prayer. Go before God and bare your heart. Express your pain. Express your sorrow. Express your desire to grow in His grace. Remember the Apostle Paul's advice in Philippians 4:4-7: *"Rejoice in the Lord always; again I will say, rejoice! Let your gentle spirit be known to all men.*

The Lord is near. Be anxious for nothing, but in everything by prayer and supplica-tion with thanksgiving let your requests be made known to God. And the peace of God, which surpasses all comprehension, will guard your hearts and minds in Christ Jesus."

"Deliver us from evil." To walk in the paths of righteousness and avoid the evil that tempts us to stray from God's ways, pray Proverbs 3:6: *"In all your ways acknowledge Him, and He will make your paths straight."*

God answers prayer three different ways:

Yes.

No.

Wait for yes or no.

The waiting or delay in answered prayer may be for a reason that God foreknows and we can't foresee.

Through faith, we work through problems incomprehensible to us. Wait can be the best answer to a prayer. We're fickle human beings and the desires of our heart change over time. The relationships, posses-sions, and abilities we desire today will not be what we want and need at a later stage in our lives. Maturity and time change us. As Steve Maraboli said, "Sometimes problems don't require a solution to solve them; in-stead they require maturity to outgrow them."

Garth Brooks sang the lyrics of "Unanswered Prayers" which re-mind us that God's "No" to our prayers may be God's greatest gift to us.

Although you will not find these words—*For Yours is the kingdom and the power and the glory forever. Amen*—at the end of the Lord's Prayer in Matthew or Luke, they have become part of the prayer through tradi-tion. The ending words complete the circle and take us back to the be-ginning to honor God.

From the Unanswerable "Why" of Crisis to the Comfort of Faith

"The journey of belief begins in the head, but it must migrate twelve inches to the south to the heart to make a difference in our lives. Why? Because we live from the heart. We live consistent with the beliefs embraced in our hearts."—Randy Frazee

Why did God let this happen to me?

Chaplains and encouragers often encounter spiritual questions from those in crisis. Crises rip us out of the contentedness and complacency of everyday life, forcing us to ask questions about the future and eternity.

Given appropriate circumstances where the questioner asks sincere questions and seeks spiritual answers, share the comfort God provides through His promises in God's Word and through the faith of other believers. In C. S. Lewis' book *The Problem of Pain*, he makes this wry observation: *"The real problem is not why some pious, humble, believing people suffer, but why some do not."*

Life throws up obstacles to those strong in faith. However, our secure knowledge of God's promise of eternal life with Him infuses us with confidence and hope. Therefore, we can persevere despite unpleasant or heartbreaking circumstances.

Useful to many people in sharing their faith in Christ, this simple letter sequence—ABCDE—outlines the way to faith from the book of Romans in the New Testament. Paul, the apostle of Jesus Christ, wrote the following Scripture verses.

A: Admit You Have Sinned

". . . for all have sinned and fall short of the glory of God . . ."
—Romans 3:23

Admitting our wrong attitudes and actions places life in perspective. As sinners, no matter what we do, we fall short of God's glory or what's best for our lives. To connect with God, we first acknowledge our sinful nature and admit our wrong doings.

But, we say, "We haven't committed terrible deeds (sin) in our lives (robbery, deceit, murder, extortion, rape, or terrorist attacks). We're not evil or sadistic." More likely, we consider ourselves "good people" trying to live "good lives" doing "good deeds" for others. But yes, we have committed more everyday garden varieties of sin: jealousy, envy, anger, selfishness, greed, lust, lying . . . .

We're not alone. In the Bible, many characters sinned, from Adam through Zedekiah, with numerous characters in between. But being in good company does not change our basic nature.

God desires a relationship with us. He created us to live in relationship with Him. Admitting our wrong attitudes and actions removes the barriers of sin between us and God. Wrongdoers receive earthly punishment for their offenses. Yet, God offers mercy and grace to the guilty, releasing us from our burdens of sin. Assurance of God's forgiveness frees us from guilt, bringing comfort and security.

B: Believe that Jesus Died for Your Sins

> *"But God demonstrates His own love toward us, in that while we were yet sinners, Christ died for us."—Romans 5:8*

Yes, while we were still sinners, Christ died for us. God's only Son, a sinless man paid the penalty for our offenses and purchased our freedom. He releases us from the power of sin and the legalism of religious law. Jesus's sacrifice paid the ransom to offer us eternal life.

C: Confess that Jesus is Lord

> *"... if you confess with your mouth Jesus as Lord, and believe in your heart that God raised Him from the dead, you will be saved; for with the heart a person believes, resulting in righteousness, and with the mouth he confesses, resulting in salvation . . . for 'Whoever will call on the name of the Lord will be saved.'"—Romans 10:9-10; 13*

God knows our hearts, and He knows when we have godly sorrow for our misdeeds. We can fool people, but we cannot fool God.

Pray: *Dear Lord, thank You for loving me even though I have sinned against You in thought, word, or deed. I am deeply sorry for those sins. I believe Jesus is the Son of God and He died on the cross to free me from my sins. Help me turn away from my sin and turn toward a life more pleasing to You. Thank You for giving me the gifts of life and Your love. Amen.*

D: Determine to Live a Godly Life

> *"For by grace you have been saved through faith; and that not of yourselves, it is the gift of God; not as a result of works, so that no one may boast. For we are His workmanship, created in Christ Jesus for good works, which God prepared beforehand so that we would walk in them."—Ephesians 2:8-10*

Repentance means to turn *from* sin and turn *toward* a change of mind and purpose in life. Our desires and actions mirror the attitudes and actions of Christ. Read these words from Philippians 4:8-9 on living a godly life. *"Finally, brothers, whatever is true, whatever is noble, whatever is right, whatever is pure, whatever is lovely, whatever is admirable—if anything is excellent or praiseworthy—think about such things. Whatever you have learned or received or heard from me, or seen in me—put it into practice. And the God of peace will be with you."*

E: Express Your Faith

> *"...grow in the grace and knowledge of our Lord and Savior Jesus Christ. To Him be the glory, both now and to the day of eternity. Amen."—2 Peter 3:18*

Tell others how God changed your life and purpose. Share God's powerful message, the promise of eternal life with God. When you confess your faith in Jesus Christ, you join many others who believe in God's sovereignty. He shepherds His people with compassionate care through good times and hard times. God's words of encouragement in the Bible soften our attitudes and help us develop stronger interpersonal relationships. His words guide us to live a life where worshipping God and caring for others takes precedence over selfishness and other lesser matters. Join with other believers in celebrating this good news.

Whenever a person at Ground Zero decided to ask Jesus into their life, I shared Scripture verses with them, prayed with them, and asked them to sign my Bible. Now when I read the portion of Scripture I used with them, I see their names, and I pray specifically for them. This brings me great joy for I know we'll meet again in heaven and share eternity together.

Appendix B: Chaplain's Toolbox: Practical How-to's

"Chaplains are ordinary people with no supernatural power of their own. But in partnership with the presence of God, chaplains bring calm to chaos, victory over despair, comfort in loss, and sufficiency in need. The very presence of the chaplain reminds the client that God is very present to them."

—Naomi K. Paget and Janet R. McCormack

This section includes insights into the preparation and training needed by emergency service workers and chaplains as well as specific strategies to minister to people in traumatic situations. A person does not become a chaplain by buying a piece of paper from an anonymous Internet source. Chaplains study God's Word and promises and stand ready at all times to offer an answer for their faith. A chaplain's prayerful presence, listening without judgment, and demonstrating faith in action leads people to seek our God of comfort Who brings healing to broken hearts.

We're not all chaplains serving in a public role, but every person can be a counselor at one time or another. The strategies in the Chaplain's Toolbox will help you care for a distraught or grieving friend, talk with a hospitalized person, or offer help someone with a chronic ailment. Counseling and friendship share many core principles: Be there. Listen. Provide for physical needs. Use comforting words. When the opportunity arises, share comfort from God's Word and pray.

Role of Chaplains

"The crosses and the clerical collars seem to be quiet reminders of hope, of divine presence, that God is still there in the midst of tragedy. Just to see the symbol of the cross is to be reminded of Christ's love."—Chaplain Ray Giunta

Chaplains play a unique role in a pluralistic society. As the institutional church in America declines, many who formerly practiced religion in red brick buildings with tall white steeples no longer do so. Children raised in traditional religious enclaves have not carried on what they learned as they matured, married, and raised their children.

Further expanding the issue of diversity, people of other faiths immigrated to our country and held onto their beliefs, and rightly so. After all, America offers freedom of religious choice and practice.

In the past, churches and other religious organizations formed communities that cared for those in physical, emotional, or spiritual crisis. With a general decline in formal religious organizations, who serves the physical, emotional, and spiritual needs of those who do not participate in organized religious activities? Who answers the questions when crises occur: *"Where is God?" "Why did this happen?" "What am I doing here?" "What is the purpose of my life?"*

One answer is chaplains. Chaplains of all faiths serve on the front lines of critical incidents in health care, military, prisons, education, corporations, and municipal police and fire departments. They also serve as first responders in crises caused by terrorist attacks, natural disasters, fires, and other emergencies. While remaining true to their faith, chaplains commit to offering compassionate care to anyone in need, regardless of religious preference.

Representative of other organization's codes, the Evangelical Free Church of America's code of ethics clearly states: "I will seek to provide pastoral care and ministry to persons of religious bodies other than my own within my area of responsibility with the same investment of myself as I give to members of my own religious body . . . . I will respect the beliefs and traditions of my colleagues and those to whom I minister,"

EFCA *Chaplains Handbook*. (Evangelical Free Church of America. www. efca.org) Although willing to assist a member of any faith, most often chaplains assist a person in finding a chaplain of their beliefs.

Chaplain Certification

"Let every man abide in the calling wherein he is called and his work will be as sacred as the work of the ministry."—A. W. Tozer

Finding credibility in ministry in today's world can be hard. When men and women alike tell me they're ordained, I ask, "Who ordained you?" Most describe their comprehensive training and the honor to represent our Lord or their faith in emergencies. A few proudly wave a card they received through the mail. For a few dollars, anyone can receive a piece of paper declaring, "You're a chaplain."

I once received a call as a chaplain to a fatal truck accident. As I approached the scene a woman rushed up to me and asked, "How do I become a chaplain?"

The accident scene shook me up, so my advice to her was brief: "Study, take classes on the Bible and counseling, spend time in prayer, and get ordained."

Being a chaplain is a serious vocation and deserves proper training and certification. I obtained my original certification in Illinois. When I moved to other states, I took more classes than I ever dreamed of to meet each state's requirements to re-earn the title of "Certified Chaplain." Every state has similar requirements, with some variation on critical incident training and post-traumatic stress training. We follow the rules of the state or area in which we work.

About a week later at the scene of another traffic incident where critical injuries occurred, the woman who'd asked about becoming a chaplain responded to the accident scene as a chaplain. I did a double take and asked, "How did you obtain a chaplain's certificate so quickly?"

"I went to my pastor," she said, "and told him of my desire to be a chaplain."

My pastor said, "Okay, I ordain you. Now go and be a chaplain."

Chaplains cringe at that story because this charade, no matter how well intentioned, waters down certified chaplains' credibility and training. The process to become an officially certified chaplain is much more time consuming and challenging.

Chaplains can be of any religious faith. Each religious denomination or organization develops chaplaincy requirements including ministerial training, certifying credentials, and guidelines for experience in ministry settings. Chaplains may represent a particular denomination, but must be ecumenical in service. Their goal is not to preach or convert, but to provide comfort and care to anyone in need.

While many theological training sites provide ministerial training for chaplains, professional organizations certify particular areas of service (e.g. religious denominations, health services, military, or penal institutions). Many organizations and individual states provide additional training for chaplains in crisis management, disaster relief, and post-traumatic stress syndrome. Basic requirements for chaplains include theological training and practical experience. For organizations sponsoring training for chaplains, see *Resources for Chaplains* in Appendix C.

Chaplain's Self-Care in Crises

"You must take care of yourself before you can help others. The ministry of compassion and caring must come from the overflow of God's compassion and caring in your life."—Janet K. Paget and Janet R. MacCormack

When working as a first responder in a major crisis, chaplains provide physical, emotional, and spiritual support to others in need, sometimes at the cost of depleting their own emotional and physical resources. While the temptation is to continue working throughout the crisis regardless of your physical needs, you must avoid doing so. Consider these suggestions to stay healthy and alert on the job.

* Eat healthy food, stay hydrated, and get enough rest.
* Take breaks from the work and the stress.
* Develop a support team on site and back at home.

* Seek counsel when the crisis seems overwhelming and stress affects your emotional well-being.

* Use your spiritual resources: prayer, Bible reading, and fellowship with other chaplains.

To serve people in the worst moments of their lives, crisis workers must be at their best performance level. Easier said than done. While working at Ground Zero, my physical, mental, and spiritual health needed to remain strong and intact. When I felt exhausted, I reminded myself that to be effective, I must be prepared. I needed food, water, rest, and spiritual uplifting.

Passionate about their work, nothing kept the working heroes on the Pile away from their search efforts. In the final moments of a recovery of human remains in the Pile or at the discovery of a firefighter's tool, they pressed on to recover the body, so they often skipped meals. At these times, everyone worked on adrenalin and kept going despite the frustrations and questionable working conditions.

On my first two tours at Ground Zero, I did the same thing. I understood that frustration, that tension, that compulsion to keep going, no matter what. When exhaustion claims us one way or another, we start to drag, get sluggish and cranky. We don't even know what time of the day it is. We slow down on the job and risk making harmful mistakes.

Intense stress took a toll on my body and my mind while working at Ground Zero, forcing me to realize I had to correct the situation. On later tours, I made it a point to eat at regular intervals, to drink a lot of water, and to get enough rest. I also spent time with other chaplains reviewing events, releasing tension, and praying. I made sure my personal well-being remained in check.

I tried to keep the wear and tear on my body to a minimum. I kept up with those young guys for just so long, then I needed a break. When physically exhausted, I was almost useless. At times, though overtired, when called upon to give emotional support to others, I asked the Lord to give me a second wind, and He was faithful to provide a surge of strength. I never received more than I could handle at any time.

At Ground Zero, I saw people on the edge of breakdown anxiety. To be available to serve when needed, I knew enough to stay healthy, rested, and alert. I didn't want to drop my marble bag or lose the cheese off my crackers, as the sayings go, and become ineffective. But once in a while, I looked around that seemingly hopeless devastation and asked myself, "Why am I here?" "Why am I working in this hopeless situation?"

When discouragement threatened to overtake my stability, I joined with other chaplains in time of reflection, prayer, and general release of frustrations. These invaluable sessions helped us form strong bonds with each other. They also enabled us to keep our work in perspective, and to keep our emotions somewhat in balance.

I also pulled out my wallet and looked at the pictures of my beautiful wife and children. "Oh, yes. That's why I'm here." Serving America meant I served my family, too. Knowing my family at home supported my work in Manhattan further encouraged me.

Hearing my wife's tender, sweet voice on the telephone at just the right times helped. She always reassured me and kept me updated on the toils of life at home. I think it was also good for her to share her problems with me in these brief phone calls and not bear the whole load alone. Sue was the core of my home support team.

After each tour at Ground Zero, I returned home and stayed in bed for hours on end to catch up on sleep. When at home, my wife, Sue, noticed my out-of-character quietness, but she was smart enough and supportive enough not to pester me about the details circulating through my mind.

Those incomprehensible scenes from New York City were almost more than I could handle, and I didn't want to lay that burden on her, too. At that point, I couldn't put my memories, thoughts, or feelings into words. How can anyone share, even with the closest family members, the human tragedies observed firsthand on the Pile? So I locked them away from my family.

At the firehouse where I worked, I took advantage of downtime between calls and rested as much as possible. Though discouraged at times, I felt supported by my firefighter workmates. No one in the firehouse ever mocked or chided me for my moodiness. Understanding the critical nature of my work, they were there to lean on. They also gave me space to work through my physical and emotional exhaustion.

To be ready at all times to help others in need, taking care of oneself is critical when working in crises.

How to Address People's Physical Needs in Crisis: I.P.D.A. Checklist

"Chaplaincy differs from being a pastor in that it is primarily a ministry of presence. Our role as a chaplain is to serve, not preach. We are a witness to our faith by our doing, caring and loving. When an officer asks why we do what we do, then the door is open to share our faith."—International Conference of Police Chaplains

A chaplain seeks to serve the spiritual needs of people, but first, we must consider the physical requirements of those we encounter. Remember the exhortation in Scripture in James 2:16: *"If a brother or sister is without clothing and in need of daily food, and one of you says to them, 'Go in peace, be warmed and be filled,' and yet you do not give them what is necessary for their body, what use is that?"* My high school driving instructor used the acronym, I.P.D.A.—Identify, Predict, Decide, and Act—to help students develop safe driving skills. But I use this acronym in ministry, too. Translated into chaplainese, the informal I.P.D.A. physical needs checklist below determines a starting place to care for those who suffer.

Identify a person who wants or needs to talk.

Sometimes a person in need of physical, emotional, or spiritual care will approach you directly, especially if you wear identification pinpointing you as a counselor or chaplain. My chaplain's hard hat and turnout gear with my name emblazoned on the back offered an unspoken invitation for confidential talk. Because we represent God, people share stories of pain they cannot share with others. Chaplains and counselors maintain strict confidentiality.

Other times, keep your eyes open for people who may be in such pain that they withdraw into themselves. They are the most fragile, and the least likely to request help. Do you see someone who spends a lot of time alone? Who avoids interaction with other people? Shuns conversation? Avoids eye contact? If so, this person needs your care and concern. Wait for an opportunity to speak, then find a point of contact, and listen carefully if the person decides to speak.

Predict if the person has a specific physical need.

Handle these issues first: safety, food and drink, shelter, clothing, medical care, and any legal issues.

1. Safety: Is the person safe? Safety was always an issue on the Pile and a conscious concern of the authorities. Smashed toes, twisted ankles, blisters, cuts, scrapes, bruises, and burns were common physical injuries. Thanks to St. Paul's volunteers and other service sites, aches and pains suffered by workers received professional attention.

What safety concerns does your counselee have? Do they suffer from physical or sexual abuse? Do they suffer from emotional abuse (yelling or verbal insults or actual threats of violence or actual violence). How can you assist in removing these threats?

Other professionals or organizations can assist you to meet these needs. In fact, a chaplain may need to make a report to the local authorities when you sense the counselee may physically hurt himself or someone else.

2. Hunger: One thing I worried about when I arrived in New York City was how my physical needs would be met. Where would I obtain food? I was blessed to connect with St. Paul's Chapel on the first day, but other local organizations provided great care of volunteers, too. I often thought about the homeless and wondered. *Who takes care of them? Who responds to their basic needs?*

Provide immediate food assistance, and then point the person to sources for food in the community: soup kitchens, food pantries, spaghetti dinners. Add the names of local churches and organizations that maintain food pantries to your resource list and refer hungry people to them. Better yet, arrange transportation to get them to food banks.

3. Homelessness: Even as a chaplain with faith in my God, I wondered upon my arrival in New York City days after 9/11: *Who will provide shelter? Where will I sleep?* The vulnerability I felt at the lack of basic needs proved to be another lesson for me. Many people lost their housing in the areas surrounding Ground Zero. Smashed windows, toxic ash, and smoke rendered their apartments uninhabitable.

My lack of planned shelter that first night helped me realize the frustration and disruption many New York City residents experienced. Homelessness was a serious concern. Where did so many displaced persons go? Thankfully, family and friends pitched in to take them in, and St. Paul's Chapel quickly provided for my needs. But what about those who are perpetually homeless? We all take too much for granted. Serving the homeless in our communities brings us face-to-face with people with physical, emotional, and spiritual needs. Perhaps abuse is an issue. Perhaps a battered woman needs a safe place for herself and her children.

4. Clothing: When my clothing disappeared at St. Paul's, I felt anxious and violated. Who took my personal belongings? What would I wear? Feelings of helplessness and vulnerability loomed their ugly heads. And again, I learned two lessons. One, our possessions become too important, and when we have none, our anxiety increases. Two, I learned to live with less and to be content with what I had.

Clothing is not the only issue. Clean clothing is essential. Homeless people do not have access to washing machines and dryers. Churches or other social groups sometimes organize wash days at local laundromats. They collect quarters from members, purchase laundry soap and other supplies, and meet homeless people at laundromats. Clean clothes lift spirits, providing encouragement to people out of work and out of money.

5. Medical Care: I felt blessed to receive medical care from volunteers at St. Paul's when needed. As chaplains, we often meet people with medical issues, so we must be aware of local programs providing services for those in need. Local Alcoholics Anonymous and Narcotics Anonymous groups provide support to addicts who want to break habits controlling their lives.

6. Legal issues: A person in crisis may be stressed due to pressing legal issues. A wife may need a protection order or counsel on separation and divorce issues. Children may need temporary foster homes. Address their immediate legal issues. Be sure to identify your community's legal aid resources and add them to your resource list.

Decide to refer for further services.

Chaplains and counselors interact with victims under severe stress. Their home just burned to the ground. A child was seriously injured in a traffic accident. An adult experienced a heart attack or a stroke. Firefighters and paramedics arrive at the crisis scene. Chaplains take care of temporary physical, emotional, and spiritual needs. After that, you may never see the person again or have an opportunity to follow up with additional services.

Encourage the victims you encounter to seek counseling and other community resources after they return home or to a safer location. When you identify serious emotional and spiritual issues, emphasize the need to continue talking about their problems with a professional. In some situations (suicidal persons), seek medical help immediately. You may save a life. If needed, medical personnel at the hospital can assist with further counseling.

Act to help in any way humanly possible.

Take action in any way humanly possible to help a person resolve their problems. Take care of physical needs before attending to spiritual needs. Don't just offer lip service, but walk the walk and talk the talk. Help the person in need, which this scriptural principle addresses in Matthew 25:34-36, 40: *"Come, you who are blessed by my Father; take your inheritance, the kingdom prepared for you since the creation of the world. For I was hungry and you gave me something to eat, I was thirsty and you gave me something to drink, I was a stranger and you invited me in, I needed clothes and you clothed me, I was sick and you looked after me, I was in prison and you came to visit me.*

The King will reply, 'I tell you the truth, whatever you did for one of the least of these brothers of mine, you did for me.'" Matthew 25:34-36, 40

How to Respond to People's Emotional and Spiritual Needs in Crisis

"Chaplaincy is above all a ministry of presence, of simply being there amid things—a sacramental ministry, not primarily in the 'churchy' sense of celebrating the sacraments but in the theological one of taking everyday stuff of life and making it a sign of God's presence and love."—Miranda Threlfall-Holmes and Mark Newitt

Paramedics Talk, Chaplains Listen

"Talker" could be my middle name. I grew up with my good friend Tony. We both loved to talk for hours about anything and everything: sports, the weather, school, friends, weekend activities, or whatever. So, as a chaplain, it's sometimes sheer torture for me to remain quiet and listen. Fortunately, as we mature, we learn to control impulsive behavior and talk less and listen more.

As a paramedic (before becoming a chaplain), I obtained information on patients in emergencies quickly to evaluate the situation and the patient's condition. If the patient was conscious, I asked rapid-fire questions hardly stopping to breathe:

Can you hear me?

What's your name?

What happened?

What medical conditions do you have?

What medications do you take?

Did you take any drugs?

Have you had any alcohol?

Paramedics make life-and-death decisions and need information quickly to analyze the problem and save a life. I needed to determine quickly whether the patient was in cardiac arrest, had blood glucose level issues, or was in an alcohol or drug-induced trauma. I worked through paramedic protocol.

Do we have to administer oxygen?

Do we use heart paddles?

Do we have to administer Narcan to reverse a drug overdose?

However, a chaplain counseling a person in distress works just the opposite: Be patient. Wait. Don't ask questions or interrupt when the person speaks. When people talked, I forced myself to slow down and concentrate on listening. Underlying problems can be elusive. Identifying an emotional or spiritual issue is often as critical as a medical issue. However, drawing out that issue takes more time to analyze.

Many times I sat in St. Paul's Chapel with someone who requested to speak to a cleric or counselor. On one end of the spectrum, I met with people who were unable to say a word. They wanted to share and open up, but they were at a loss for words. This was common. In those cases, I prayed silently for them and waited for them to articulate their deep pain.

When something lies heavy on a counselee's mind, you can't begin a session with cheerful banter. That belittles your purpose. You're there to bring comfort to a suffering person, but first you need to understand the nature of their difficulties. Be still and wait.

My goal was to be a good listener and not to coach distressed persons on what to say. I repeated in my head, "Just be a listener and wait for this person to open up. Do not form a question. When the person speaks, wait until they finish speaking. Rephrase what the person tells you to ensure you understand. Pause to process the dialogue before you speak."

On the other end of the spectrum, some people verbalize everything without hesitation. Anger. Sorrow. Frustration. Guilt. Remorse. Regret. Yes, and sometimes they use offensive language, but that hardly matters. Counselors and chaplains frequently hear that kind of language. It doesn't shock us.

We look past the cursing for the deeper problem. Once the barrage stops, the person in crisis reaches a calmer state and communicates more clearly. Often people under stress just need to talk to someone who'll sit and listen.

Casual conversations at Ground Zero were not the norm of life. Yes, in life we experience tragedies, but not of that magnitude. People watched the collapse of the World Trade Center towers on TV or from the ground as loved ones or friends died in front of their eyes. Filled with despair, they were unable to turn away. Helpless and hopeless, sometimes they vomited. Retelling these emotional events sometimes brought back physical symptoms.

At the Pile, on the perimeter, and at St. Paul's, we chaplains listened for long periods of time to give workers and volunteers the opportunity to bare their souls. At times, the terror of their stories or the pain displayed left me speechless, and I wept with them. Tears can be loud and resounding and healing for both counselee and counselor. Oh yes, at times, I wanted to interject some golden nugget of my personal wisdom. To keep my attention on listening to the person, I pretended that duct tape covered my mouth.

This is why chaplains need training to learn the different situations and struggles people experience when they suffer. It's imperative to learn how to be flexible and to avoid doing more harm by throwing out callous responses or quick-fix solutions.

How to L.I.S.T.E.N. to People in Crisis: 6 Practical Tips

Once you help resolve physical needs, listen carefully to sort out emotional and spiritual issues. In real estate, the major slogan for buying a home is "Location. Location. Location." In ministry, as a pastor, chaplain, or counselor, we say, "Listen. Listen. Listen."

Listening is a critical skill in counseling, however, be flexible. Counseling a person is not like following a flow chart: If this, then do that. Each counselee has different needs and responds to different approaches. Some wind up slowly to spill their personal issues. Others from word one spout off their problems. Still others remain silent, unable to formulate their words. Your job is to be flexible and determine the best approach, which begins with "Be still and wait."

Listen.

Be a good listener to all persons, but especially to a crisis victim who speaks in repetitive or rambling thoughts. Don't assume that when they stop talking they've given you all the information you need, or they've expressed all their concerns. Asking, "Is there anything else you want to tell me?" often draws out more of their concerns.

Restate what the person tells you to ensure you understand. Pause to process the dialogue. When they're finished sharing if you need more information, formulate questions.

"You are upset because . . . ?"

"You feel angry because . . . ?"

Initiate.

When a person needs more time to reveal their issues, initiate a conversation to identify where they're at emotionally and to show you care. If the conversation is informal, find a point of contact. Do they have children? Pets? Live in a nearby neighborhood? Attend the same church? Get them talking, then ease them toward areas of concern.

Stay.

Stay to learn about their family, friends, interests, activities, feelings. Ask about their favorite band or singers or their favorite sport or activity. Let them talk about things in general instead of the specific traumatic event affecting them in the moment. Connect with them first. They may not be ready to talk about the harder things.

Take quality time.

Don't just say, "Hello" and run. Help the distressed person triumph over crisis. Building a trusting relationship takes time. When someone asks you for a few minutes of your time, be prepared to give much more. In cases where you're limited in time, focus your attention. Do the best you can with the time available, then encourage the person to seek follow-up counseling. Ask, "Do you know a pastor or counselor you can talk to?" Get them to commit to a follow-up action. Finally, hold them up in prayer.

Equip them.

If appropriate and with permission, equip them with prayer or Scripture to meditate on. Or share a hymn, a poem, a song, or Bible verse to soothe them. These verses might help: *"Do not fear, for I am with you; do not be dismayed, for I am your God. I will strengthen you and help you; I will uphold you with my righteous right hand."* (Isaiah 41:10) *"In God alone my soul is at peace, from Him I receive help."* (Psalm 62:2)

Notify authorities.

If you sense serious issues or potential suicide or threats of harm to themselves or others, you may save a life by referring this person to medical and psychiatric assistance.

How to Respond to Suffering and Grief

"Knowing the Lord and His comfort does not take away the ache; instead, it supports you in the middle of the ache."—Bill Dunn and Kathy Leonard

Terrorist attacks on New York City and Washington D.C. created an instant need for hundreds of qualified chaplains and counselors. Although some people at Ground Zero did not want to hear about God or faith, many others felt compelled to ask spiritual questions. They'd gone along day-to-day without considering their eternal future and now the possibility of sudden death confronted them face-to-face. This terrorist attack brought the realization to all of us: Life is temporary, and we must explore the question of eternity now.

Pastors, chaplains, and counselors minister to those who grieve. How can each of us help? As friends and associates, we also have opportunities to minister to others who grieve or suffer in some way. After all, friends see others suffering long before it comes to the attention of trained professionals.

How Do People Grieve?

"The worst kind [of crying] happened when your soul wept and no matter what you did, there was no way to comfort it. A section withered and became a scar on the part of your soul that survived."—Katie McGarry

Grievers suffer losses that family members and bystanders cannot fathom unless they've suffered similar losses. Even then, grief responses are different depending on the degree of relationship or dysfunction between the deceased and the mourner. A spouse grieves harder for a deceased partner than for a distant uncle. Sadness for the uncle isn't life altering. Grieving for a spouse or a child is life shattering.

Mourners experience roller-coaster emotions: steep climbs and sudden drops, highs and lows, sharp curves and jolting bends. Some hill-crests are higher and steeper; others lower, longer, and flatter. The hills don't level out until the end of the run when the car pulls into the disembarking zone.

At times, a griever's emotions feel out-of-control, and the intensity frightens the griever. Hysterical crying, temper tantrums, extreme mood swings, or withdrawal can scare family members and friends.

Many characters in the Bible grieved deeply for personal losses. Consider Rachel in Matthew 2. *"A voice is heard in Ramah* [a small town north of Jerusalem], *weeping and great mourning, Rachel weeping for her children and refusing to be comforted, because they are no more."* (Matthew 2:18) This sorrow, prophesied in Jeremiah 31:15, struck after Herod ordered soldiers to kill every baby boy two years old and under in and around Bethlehem. Herod attempted to find and kill the baby the three kings from the east called the "King of the Jews." The Living Bible describes Rachel's mourning this way: *"Screams of anguish come from Ramah, weeping unrestrained; Rachel weeping for her children, uncomforted—for they are dead."*

Grievers recognize these reactions. They experience them. Screams of anguish. Unrestrained weeping. Being beyond comfort.

While many persons who have suffered losses do not go through every extreme emotional reaction, many do. And some suffer in solitary silence, withdrawn into an inner hell of torment.

When others return to normal routines, the griever's 'new normal' struggles with complex issues and emotions. However fear, loneliness, and helplessness possess and paralyze the grieving person.

Like powerful ocean waves, grief sweeps over the mourner. At first, tsunami-sized waves roll in frequent and hard. Over time the intensity of waves and the frequency lessen. Even so, unexpected waves of sorrow overwhelm the mourner.

Grievers fear their deceased loved one will be forgotten. They're replaced at work and in social groups, but they can never be replaced in the griever's heart. Even if a spouse remarries, or a mother births another child, they don't replace or fill the void of the one who died.

Holidays and other special occasions present special problems. Dates on the calendar stir up anxiety. Every "first" triggers pain and memories. Birthdays. Anniversaries. Holidays. Graduations. Weddings. Births of grandchildren. Each and every year, every exciting occasion of that loved one's past life returns as a painful, cherished memory to a broken-hearted person. Memories of more joyful times on these occasions and lost dreams of the future cause grievers to mourn anew.

Moving through mourning is hard work. Life, irreversibly changed, is lonelier and more difficult without the loved one.

How to Help a Grieving Person

"Deep grief sometimes is almost like a specific location, a coordinate on a map of time. When you are standing in that forest of sorrow, you cannot imagine that you could ever find your way to a better place. But if someone can assure you that they themselves have stood in that same place, and now have moved on, sometimes this will bring hope."—Elizabeth Gilbert

Chaplains and pastors counsel people who are grieving, but close friends can also fulfill this role. Other friends may offer temporary comfort, but long-term, trusted friends make the difference between emotional survival and clinical depression. What you say is critical to a person who suffers. How can we offer our God of hope to people in crisis?

Sit and wait. When a grieving person cannot bear comfort, you must sit and wait, just as Job's friends sat with him and waited seven days, saying nothing, before speaking to him about his suffering. (Job 1:13) When Job managed to speak, he lamented: *"If only my anguish could be weighed and all my misery be placed on the scales! It would surely outweigh the sand of the seas. . . ."* (Job 6:2-3) *"My eyes will never see happiness again."* (Job 7:7)

Listen from the heart. Our first charge is to understand that grieving is complex and to listen carefully when the grieving person speaks. The grieving person may repeat the same stories over and over or describe in detail the sequence of the illness or the accident causing the death. It's normal for these stories to echo constantly through the griever's mind.

Share memories about their loved one. During the memorial service family and friends tell tearful stories of their memories of the deceased person. However afterward, people rarely mention the name of the deceased for fear of arousing emotional pain. Yet, not hearing the name causes equal pain. Grievers crave hearing their loved one's name and yearn to hear more stories about their lives. They want to remember the details of their life, not forget them.

Give the gift of time. Understand that the person mourning cannot respond in normal ways. Extreme mood swings, confusion, and sudden fits of crying are normal. And remember, they will never be the same person they were before their loved one's death.

Respect the grieving person's right for privacy. Let them grieve in the manner they choose, but do not forget them. They still need your comfort and compassion, even though they may seem to reject it. Invite them to participate in your social events. Take them to lunch. Drop by to see how they're faring.

Be a friend now and for the long run. After emotional events such as the death of a loved one, relationships and old friendships sometimes become strained. Other family members and bystanders simply can't understand the depths of emotional pain the grieving person suffers. They feel uncomfortable. They don't know what to say, so they stay away. Be courageous and spend quality time with the suffering person.

Offer practical acts of kindness. Help the grieving person face each new task. Help them make funeral arrangements, pay bills, do laundry, cook, and clean. All these tasks are insurmountable at first, but a little help from a friend shrinks the tasks to a manageable size.

Send cards but add a personal touch. Circle or underline key words to show you've carefully selected the card. Add a personal note. Send "Thinking of you" greetings from time to time. People who grieve often think their friends have forgotten them. Your card or note reassures them that they're not forgotten. Send index cards with encouraging Bible verses.

Provide a healthy meal. Keep in mind that not everyone likes tuna-noodle casseroles or pasta dishes.

Offer transportation to appointments. Grief consumes the brain's resources and focus. Driving in traffic adds to their stress. Transport them to their appointment and then treat them to a meal. They need a break and some company.

Encourage grieving people to seek community support groups or individual counseling. The grieving person may benefit from counseling or connecting with others who experienced a similar loss. When appropriate, ask if they've considered talking to a counselor or pastor, or joining a grief recovery group. Provide names and addresses of counselors or grief groups obtained from people who've experienced the same type of loss. Check out support groups such as Griefshare (griefshare.org/hope) or TAPS (www.taps.org). These organizations help mourners identify with others going through the same struggles.

How to Speak from the Heart

"The reality is that you will grieve forever. You will not 'get over' the loss of a loved one; you will learn to live with it. You will heal and you will rebuild yourself around the loss you have suffered. You will be whole again but you will never be the same. Nor should you be the same nor would you want to."—Elisabeth Kübler-Ross

Initially, say as few words as possible when first encountering a person who's suffered the loss of a loved one. "I am sorry for your loss." Offer to pray with the grieving person if the person accepts your offer, and you feel comfortable praying with them. The grieving person may not remember what you say, but they'll remember the time you prayed with them. In your prayer, redirect their view from hopelessness to the hope we have in our heavenly Father.

Ask if you can share your memories of their loved one. Family members and friends fear stirring up the grieving person's emotions, so they avoid talking about the deceased person. In reality, the grieving person longs to talk about their lost loved one. Share favorite pictures. Share favorite foods. Cry and laugh together as you share treasured memories.

Choose your words thoughtfully. There are appropriate things to say to a suffering person, and there are inappropriate things to say. Think about your life. Do you remember hurtful things said to you, sometimes deliberately, sometimes innocently, that provoked pain?

What you say may not be meant to be hurtful. However, if the person who suffers hears insensitive platitudes or advice, you may have just lost a friend forever. When dealing with the worst emotional pain of their lives, people in crisis lose the ability to evaluate your intent. The inappropriate things you say burn deep into their fragile emotions, ingraining the pain into their memory.

Speaking to the grieving person when you meet them in casual situations can be difficult. Ignoring the situation is callous and disheartening. The grieving person thinks you've forgotten the deceased already. Commenting on the situation, while it may bring fresh tears or pain, is better. Reminding the grieving person that the person they lost is still in your thoughts comforts them.

What Not to Say: Comments That May Trigger Pain

"I have heard many things like these; miserable comforters are you all! Will your long-winded speeches never end?"—Job 16:2

Job, a godly man of Old Testament times, suffered great losses. His children died in natural disasters. He lost his livelihood and wealth through enemy attacks. His well-intentioned friends offered support with their presence during seven days of silence, but then, they offered Job explanations for his sufferings along with advice.

Job wisely reprimanded them for trying to find explanations for his suffering. "A lot of good they are to me—those worn-out wretches!" Ultimately, Job realized his need to trust God in his suffering. Indeed, the Lord blessed Job more in the second half of his life than in the first. What useless comments and advice do we offer those who mourn? Consider these examples.

"It's going to be okay." The grieving person thinks, "It's not okay. It will never be okay again. I am angry and hurt and nothing can comfort me now. Please don't even try, just leave me alone." Like the grieving Rachel in Matthew 2, the pain is too great to embrace comfort.

"How are you?" This question is more like "How are you since the last time I saw you?" This question implies nothing big has happened. General superficial questions like this are not helpful. People sometimes don't even listen for an answer because "How are you?" is just one of those polite phrases you throw out in casual meetings.

The suffering person knows you asked this simply because you're in an awkward spot and don't know what else to say. They may respond, "I'm okay," when their world is falling apart. Their feelings remain in shambles. Mourners learn to paste on a smile and respond platitude to platitude: "I'm fine. It's going to be okay."

The griever thinks, *"It's not okay. It will never be okay again. I am angry and hurt and nothing can help me now. Please don't even try to comfort me, just leave me alone."*

Put this in perspective. A person tragically loses a whole family in an accident or the twins die in a fire (heaven forbid). A bystander (worse yet, a local news person) asks, "How do you feel?"

Really? How do you think I feel? I just had a major heartbreak or loss, and you ask me that? Are you crazy? What do you expect me to say?

Chaplains and counselors ask, "How are you holding up?" That gentler question shows more feeling and compassion for the grieving person and acknowledges the person's suffering, which is normal and expected. When tears flow with this question, give them a hug. Your presence brings comfort to those who suffer.

"I know how you feel." No, you don't. You may or may not have suffered through the same difficulty. If you haven't, you don't understand the depth of turmoil that results when a loved one dies, develops a debilitating illness, becomes handicapped, or falls under the influence of drugs or alcohol. Everyone experiences grief and sadness in different ways and you cannot be sure your feelings are the same. Yes, there are similarities, but you cannot know how they feel.

"Time will heal your sorrow." Don't tell someone suffering raw emotional pain this feeling will pass with time. I know folks who are in deep mourning twenty, thirty years later after the death of a child or loss of a spouse or parent, or a tragic accident, or other traumatic event. Mourning is an unending journey that will only be healed in heaven. We cannot put time constraints on people's pain. How dare we even think that?

"You'll get over it." "Move on." Telling someone to 'get over their loss or pain' or 'move on' minimizes the reality of their suffering and forces them to hide their pain, paste on a plastic smile, and build a façade of dishonest pleasantness, only making their mourning harder.

"You're young. You can remarry." This comment is insulting to the memory of the lost spouse and causes wincing pain. Have you forgotten my spouse already? Is he a commodity that can be so easily replaced?

"You can have another child." Yes, that's a physical possibility, true, a dead child is not replaceable. Even if the grieving person bears another child, that dead child is never forgotten. Parents who miscarried carry sorrow with them throughout their lives. They may not talk about or think about their loss on a daily basis, but they remember.

"At least he didn't suffer." "At least he didn't suffer a long time." "At leasts…" and "If onlys…" hurt even when the griever knows them to be true. "Windy words" like these do not help. They just fill air space and have no purpose. Do not try to make a positive spin on a person's death. That's not possible or appreciated.

"At least you don't have my problems." Don't recite your personal laundry list of woes to a mourner who barely has the emotional margin to survive each day. Everyone experiences trouble in this life, and we can all list our personal woes. But dumping your list on a grieving friend drains them of the emotional energy they need to survive. Their pain is too raw and they don't have the emotional strength to console you. And listing your problems minimizes their current struggles. If you can't think of anything else to say, stop talking.

"If only she'd taken better care of herself." Don't criticize or judge the deceased person. Yes, the deceased person may have contributed to their problems. Perhaps they didn't follow doctor's orders or they skipped prescribed medications, or ate the wrong foods, or avoided exercise, or were careless or reckless, or any other common mistakes. This is not a time to analyze what you think caused their death. Keep it to yourself. Of course, we acknowledge our spouse or loved one lacked discipline in some areas. Don't we all? But pointing out any faults now serves no purpose.

"Here's how I fixed this problem." "This is what you should

do." Don't give unsolicited advice. Grieving and suffering people must process through their pain before they can begin to pick up the pieces. Unwanted and undesired advice is downright obnoxious and uncaring and causes further hurt.

"You look terrible. Are you getting enough sleep?" Sleep? Normal sleep patterns become nonexistent. Lying awake, thinking and remembering, for hours at a time is the new norm. Negative comments reflect your impatience and lack of caring for the grieving person.

"Your problems are wearing me down." Grieving is not about you. If you can't say something supportive, don't say anything at all.

"Get over it." "Get a grip." "Stop complaining and get a life." "You should be over this by now." "You need to move on with your life." Grief is not a headache, a stomachache, or the flu. Temporary ailments can be cured by taking medication or drinking enough fluids or resting. No medical prescription can cure grief and sorrow has no time limits.

"It was meant to be." "It is in God's timing." "He's with God." "She's in a better place." "He's resting in peace." Don't throw out religious platitudes. They offend nonbelievers and believers alike.

Grieving is hard, hard work. When a death occurs, be there for your family members and friends. Offer your presence and prayers. Show compassion and offer a hug. Then keep the grieving person in your thoughts, prayers, and actions.

Appendix C: Recommended Resources

"We must learn to regard people less in the light of what they do or omit to do, and more in the light of what they suffer."—Dietrich Bonhoeffer

If God is all-powerful, all-knowing, and all-loving, why does suffering exist? Michael Ramsden tackles the ancient quandry of suffering. Ramsden is the International Director of RZIM and joint Director of the Oxford Centre for Christian Apologetics. Brought up in the Middle East in a Muslim culture, Michael later moved to England where he worked for the Lord Chancellor's department investing funds. While doing research in Law and Economics at Sheffield University, he taught Moral Philosophy and lectured for the International Seminar for Jurisprudence and Human Rights in Strasbourg. He has been a Professor-in-Residence at the Wolfsberg Executive Institute in Switzerland, has lectured in the White House, addressed leaders at NATO HQ in Brussels, members of the European Parliament, as well as bankers and investment managers.

God of Love, God of Judgment
   URL: www.youtube.com/watch?v=qUazX6wJPgo
God of Love, World of Suffering? 1
   URL: www.youtube.com/watch?v=EZV9G4XIHPM
God of Love, World of Suffering? 2
   URL: www.youtube.com/watch?v=peJC_IaQoz4
God of Love, World of Suffering? 3
   URL: www.youtube.com/watch?v=nR5V09_C3kM
God of Love: Church of Arrogance
   URL: www.youtube.com/watch?v=u9SnjVkWHhE
One God, Many Paths
   URL: www.youtube.com/watch?v=ni70-Knafho
Why Does God Allow Suffering?
   URL: www.vimeo.com/122101396

Resources for Chaplains

Chavez, Marshall, *What Is a Chaplain? A Military Chaplain Answers Frequently Asked Questions*, Kindle book, 2015.

Evangelical Free Church Association Chaplains Handbook URL: https://go.efca.org/

Threlfall-Holmes, Miranda and Newitt, Mark. *Being a Chaplain*. London: Society for Promoting Christian Knowledge, 2011.

Nouwen, Henri J.M., *The Wounded Healer: Ministry in Contemporary Society*. New York: Image Books, Doubleday, 1979.

Paget, Naomi K., McCormack, Janet R. *The Work of the Chaplain*. Valley Forge, PA: 2006.

Threlfall-Holmes, Miranda and Newitt, Mark. *Being a Chaplain*. London: Society for Promoting Christian Knowledge, 2011.

Toole, Mary M., *Handbook for Chaplains: Comfort My People*, New York, Paulist Press, 2006.

Woodward, Whit. *Ministry of Presence: Biblical Insight on Christian Chaplaincy*. North Fort Myers, FL: Faithful Life Publishers, 2011.

Chaplains and Counseling Organizations

American Association of Christian Counselors (AACC):
    URL: www.aacc.net/
American Association of Pastoral Counselors (AAPC):
    URL: www.aapc.org
Archdiocese for the Military Service USA:
    URL: www.milarch.org/site/
Association for Clinical Pastoral Education (ACPE):
    URL: www.acpe.edu
Association of Professional Chaplains (APC):
    URL: http://www.professionalchaplains.org
Canadian Association for Spiritual Care (CASC):
    URL: www.spiritualcare.ca
Archdiocese for the Military Service USA:
    URL: www.milarch.org/site/

Evangelical Free Church Association Chaplains:
        URL: https://go.efca.org/
Hindu Chaplaincy:
        URL: www.hinduchaplaincy.com/main.html
International Association of Christian Chaplains (IACC):
        URL: www.christianchaplains.com/
International Conference of Police Chaplains:
        URL: www.icpc4cops.org/
International Fellowship of Chaplains, Inc.:
        URL: www.ifoc.org
Jewish Chaplains Council—JCC Association:
        URL: www.jcca.org/jwb/
Muslim Chaplains:
        URL: www.associationofmuslimchaplains.com/
National Association of Catholic Chaplains (NACC):
        URL: www.nacc.org
National Association of College and University Chaplains:
        URL: www.nacuc.net/standards
National Association of Jewish Chaplains (NAJC):
        URL: www.najc.org

Military Chaplains
Military Chaplains Association:
        URL: www.mca-usa.org/
U.S. Air Force:
        URL: www.airforce.com/careers/specialty-careers/chaplain
U.S. Army Chaplains:
        URL: http://chaplainregiment.org/
U.S. Coast Guard:
        URL: www.uscg.mil/d8/command/chaplains.asp
U.S. Marines:
        URL: www.hqmc.marines.mil/Agencies/
        ChaplainoftheMarineCorps.aspx
Health Care Chaplaincy Network:
        URL: www.healthcarechaplaincy.org/
American Correctional Chaplains Association:
        URL: www.correctionalchaplains.org/

Educational Organizations

Christian Counseling & Educational Foundation (CCEF)
Provides resources on counseling and training for biblical counseling.
URL: www.ccef.org/
Narramore Christian Foundation
URL: http://ncfliving.org

Crisis Intervention/Crisis Response Training

American Association of Christian Counselors (AACC):
AACC Crisis Response Series–CRTC 102: Acute Stress, Grief and Trauma Training–12-Hour DVD Training.
URL: www.aacc.net
National Organization for Victim Assistance NOVA:
URL: www.trynova.org
International Critical Incident Stress foundation ICISF:
URL: www.ICISF.org
Christian Addiction Recovery Programs Addictions Victorious:
URL: www.addvicinc.org/
Celebrate Recovery:
URL: www.celebraterecovery.com
Reformers Unanimous
URL: www.addictionhelp4u.com/programs/addicted-2

Post-Traumatic Stress Disorder (PTSD)

Post-traumatic Stress Disorder can occur after traumatic events such as a terrorist attack, war, assault, abuse, neglect or natural disaster. Persons suffering from PTSD experience recurrent memories of the event (nightmares, flashbacks, insomnia) along with physical symptoms (anxiety, sweating, heart palpitations, nausea, shakiness in hands and legs, trouble sleeping, short temper, agitation, difficulty concentrating and completing tasks). Those suffering from PTSD may fall into substance abuse, depression, and suicidal thinking. Get help for PTSD from mental health professionals.
National Center for PTSD:
URL: www.ptsd.va.gov/

National Institute of Mental Health:

> **URL:** www.nimh.nih.gov/health/topics/post-traumatic-stress-disorder-ptsd/index.shtml

HelpGuide Organization:

> **URL:** www.helpguide.org/articles/ptsd-trauma/post-traumatic-stress-disorder.htm

GallantFew:

> **URL:** www.gallantfew.org

GallantFew, Inc. coaches, mentors and networks veterans to help them transition to civilian lives filled with hope and purpose. Founded by veterans to veterans, GallantFew's mission is to prevent veteran isolation by connecting new veterans with hometown veteran mentors, thereby facilitating a peaceful, successful transition from military service to a civilian life.

If you need help, make the call. PLEASE DO NOT TAKE ACTION OF ANY SORT until you talk to:

Phone: Army veteran Karl Monger at 817-600-0514

Phone: Army veteran Clarence Matthews at 843-697-0739

Log online to email GallantFew: www.gallantfew.org/contact/

Facebook: www.facebook.com/gallantfew

Twitter: www.twitter.com/gallantfew

YouTube: www.youtube.com/user/GallantFewInc

Address: P.O. Box 1157, Roanoke, TX 76262

Vets4Warriors:

> **URL:** www.vets4warriors.com

Vets4Warriors provides 24/7 confidential, stigma-free peer support by veterans to active duty, National Guard and reserve service members, veterans, retirees, and their families and caregivers. All calls are confidential. No information is shared with military branches or units. Vets4Warriors are available to service members and their families who do not want to engage in mental health counseling, as well as, those who currently receive counseling, but need additional support.

Phone: 855-838-8255 Toll Free, available 24 hours a day, 7 days a week for all service members in the U.S.

If serving outside the United States: Call the Global DSN Operator at: DSN 312-560-1110 (Be sure to dial as a DSN number only) or Commercial: 719-567-1110.

Email: Info@Vets4Warriors.com

Log online and chat: www.vets4warriors.com/about/contact.html

Facebook: https://www.facebook.com/Vets4Warriors

Team Rubicon:

　　　URL: www.teamrubiconusa.org

Team Rubicon unites the skills and experiences of military veterans with first responders to rapidly deploy emergency response teams. Team Rubicon's primary mission provides disaster relief to those affected by natural disasters, be it domestic or international. By pairing the skills and experiences of military veterans with first responders, medical professionals, and technology solutions, Team Rubicon aims to provide the greatest service and impact possible.

Through continued service, Team Rubicon seeks to provide our veterans with three things they lose after leaving the military: a purpose, gained through disaster relief; community, built by serving with others; and self-worth, from recognizing the impact one individual can make.

Coupled with leadership development and other opportunities, Team Rubicon looks to help veterans transition from military to civilian life. The driving force behind all of Team Rubicon's operational activity is service above self. Our actions are characterized by the constant pursuit to prevent or alleviate human suffering and to restore human dignity—we help people on their worst days.

Log online to email Team Rubicon: www.teamrubiconusa.org/contact-us

Phone: 310-640-8787

Facebook: www.facebook.com/teamrubicon

Twitter: www.twitter.com/teamrubicon

Instagram: www.instagram.com/teamrubicon

Vimeo: www.vimeo.com/channels/teamrubicon

YouTube: www.youtube.com/user/teamrubiconusa

Google+: www.plus.google.com/+TeamrubiconusaOrg/posts

Address: National Headquarters, 6171 Century Blvd. Suite 310, Los Angeles, CA 90045

The Tragedy Assistance Program for Survivors:
URL: www.taps.org

The Tragedy Assistance Program for Survivors (TAPS) offers compassionate care to all those grieving the death of a loved one who served in our Armed Forces. Since 1994, TAPS has provided comfort and hope 24 hours a day, seven days a week through a national peer support network and connection to grief resources, all at no cost to surviving families and loved ones. TAPS has assisted over 50,000 surviving family members, casualty officers, and caregivers.

TAPS serves ALL survivors: adult children, children, ex-spouses, extended family, friends and battle buddies, grandparents, parents, siblings, widows/widowers/widowed and significant others through survivor grief seminars, suicide survivor grief seminars, retreats, expeditions, 'inner warrior' events and an online community.

The TAPS Military and Veteran Caregiver Network provides pre- and post-9/11 era military and veteran caregivers with peer support and partners to reduce their isolation and increase their sense of connectedness, engagement, hopefulness, wellness and their knowledge and skills. 800 Phone Number: If you just need someone to talk to, please call TAPS any time at 1.800.959.TAPS (8277). The TAPS survivor care team can also tell you about services and programs you might find helpful. The TAPS resource and information helpline is available 24 hours a day, 7 days a week, 365 days a year.

Phone: 202-588-TAPS (8277) FAX: 571-385-2524

Facebook: www.facebook.com/TAPS4America

Twitter: www.twitter.com/TAPS4America

YouTube: www.youtube.com/supporttaps

Address: National Headquarters. 3033 Wilson Boulevard, Suite 630, Arlington, VA 22201

September 11 and Military Memorials

The Healing Field Flag Displays

This annual 9/11 Memorial honors those who lost their lives in the terrorist attacks of September 11, 2001 with a field of flags. Numerous cities honor the fallen with this dramatic and somber display.

URL: www.healingfield.org/

Field of Honor Flag Displays Military

URL: www.healingfield.org/

Recognizes the men and women who paid the ultimate price for freedom while serving our country in the military.

Bibliography

Axwell, Chris, "You, Yes You, Need to Get Counseling." *Christianity Today*. February, 2015.

Benfante, Michael, *Reluctant Hero*. New York: Skyhorse Publishing, 2011.

Bernstein, Richard, *Out of the Blue: The Story of September 11, 2001, From Jihad to Ground Zero*. New York: Henry Holt, 2002.

DiMarco, Damon, *Tower Stories, An Oral History of 9/11*, Santa Monica, CA: Santa Monica Press, 2007.

Dunn, Bill and Kathy Leonard, *Through a Season of Grief: Devotions for your Journey from Mourning to Joy*. Nashville: Thomas Nelson, 2004.

Dwyer, Jim and Flynn, Kevin, *102 Minutes: The Untold Story of the Fight to Survive Inside the Twin Towers*. New York: Times Books, 2005.

Gardner Trulson, Jennifer, *Where You Left Me*. New York: Gallery Books, 2011.

Guinta, Ray, *God @ Ground Zero: How Good Overcame Evil… One Heart at a Time*. Nashville, TN: Integrity Publishers, 2002.

Guzman-McMillan, Genelle and William Croyle, *Angel in the Rubble: The Miraculous Rescue of 9/11's Last Survivor*. New York, Howard Books, 2011.

Haskin, Leslie, *Between Heaven and Ground Zero: One Woman's Struggle for Survival and Faith in the Ashes of 9/11*. Minneapolis, Minnesota: Bethany House, 2006.

Keegan, William, Jr. Closure: *The Untold Story of The Ground Zero Recovery Mission*. New York: Simon & Schuster, 2006.

Keller, Timothy, *Walking with God through Pain and Suffering*. New York: Riverhead Books, 2013.

Luft, Benjamin J, *We're Not Leaving: 9/11 Responders Tell Their Stories of Courage, Sacrifice, and Renewal*. New York: Greenpoint Press, 2011.

MacIntosh, Mike, *When Your Life Falls Apart: Life Lessons from a Ground Zero Chaplain*. Colorado Springs, CO: Victor, 2002.

Manning, Lauren, *Unmeasured Strength*. New York: Henry Holt, 2011.

Martin S. J., James, *Searching for God at Ground Zero*. Chicago: Sheed & Ward, 2002.

National Commission on Terrorist Attacks upon the United States, *The 9/11 Commission report. Final Report of the National Commission on Terrorist Attacks upon the United States.* New York: Norton.

Piper, John and Justin Taylor, *Suffering and the Sovereignty of God.* Wheaton, Illinois: Crossway Books, 2006.

Powlison, David, *Stress: Peace Amid Pressure.* Philipsburg, NJ: Resources for Changing Lives, 2004.

Powlison, David. *Why Me? Comfort for the Victimized.* Philipsburg, NJ: Resources for Changing Lives, 2004.

Port Authority of N.Y. and N. J. Press Release, August 29, 2011, #108. Opening Ceremony - 9/11 Memorial and Museum on site of Ground Zero.

Port Authority of N.Y. and N.J. Press Release, Feb 25, 2013, #25 20th Year Commemoration service in memory and honor of six lives lost and 1000 injured in 1993 World Trade Center bombing; held at St. Peter's Roman Catholic Church in Lower Manhattan.

Smith, Dennis, *Report from Ground Zero.* New York: Plume Books, 2003.

Summers, Anthony and Swan, Robbyn. *The Eleventh Day: The Full Story of 9/11 and Osama Bin Laden.* New York: Ballantine Books, 2011.

Trulson, Jennifer Gardner, *Where You Left Me.* New York: Gallery Books, 2011.

Wright, N. T., *Into God's Presence: Prayer in the New Testament*, ed. R.L. Longenecker. 2001, Grand Rapids, Eerdmans

Websites

About 3 World Trade Center:
    URL: www.wtc.com/about/buildings/3-world-trade-center
Ground Zero Chaplain:
    URL: www.huffingtonpost.com/news/ground-zero-chaplain/
Faith and Doubt at Ground Zero:
    URL: www.pbs.org/wgbh/pages/frontline/shows/faith/etc/script.html
Remembering September 11, 2001:
    URL: www.panynj.gov/wtcprogress/events-091101.html
911 Memorial Timeline:

URL: http://www.timeline.911memorial.org/#Timeline/2
(pictorial)

September 11 Fast Facts:
URL: www.cnn.com/2013/07/27/us
september-11-anniversary-fast-facts/

Three Ominous Words of Jesus Emerge at Ground Zero:
URL: www.wnd.com/2015/10/
ominous-jesus-quote-emerges-in-ground-zero-wreckage/

World Trade Center: Timeline of Rebuilding Effort:
URL: http://www.panynj.gov/wtcprogress/timeline-rebuild
ing-effort.html

Dangerous Worksite:
URL: www.osha.gov/Publications/WTC/dangerous_worksite.
html

911 Death and Injury Total Still Rising:
URL: www.usatoday.com/story/news/2015/09/09/911-death
-and-injury-total-still-rising/71943340/

34192427R00154

Made in the USA
Middletown, DE
11 August 2016